potty train your child in just one day

PROVEN SECRETS OF THE POTTY PRO

Teri Crane

with Toni Robino

A FIRESIDE BOOK

Published by Simon & Schuster

New York London Toronto Sydney

FIRESIDE
Rockefeller Center
1230 Avenue of the Americas
New York, NY 10020

FIRESIDE and colophon are registered trademarks
of Simon & Schuster, Inc.

For information regarding special discounts for bulk purchases,
please contact Simon & Schuster Special Sales at 1-800-456-6798
or business@simonandschuster.com

Designed by Jill Weber and Joy O'Meara

Manufactured in the United States of America

1   3   5   7   9   10   8   6   4   2

Library of Congress Cataloging-in-Publication Data

Crane, Teri.
Potty train your child in just one day : proven secrets of the potty pro /
Teri Crane with Toni Robino.
    p.   cm.
"A Fireside book."
Includes bibliographical references.
1. Toilet training.   I. Robino, Toni.   II. Title.
HQ770.5.C73 2006
649'.62—dc22   2006040904

ISBN-13: 978-0-7432-7313-8
ISBN-10:   0-7432-7313-3

To my parents, Tom and Pat, for encouraging me
to never settle for less than my dreams.

contents

foreword

"You can lead a horse to water but you can't make it drink." The same idea applies to toilet training. Children need a worthwhile reason to be trained, since they're giving up the convenience of going anytime, anywhere, and the personal attention garnered by having Mom or Dad change their wet or soiled diapers.

There are a number of ways to motivate and teach toddlers, but one of the most effective is "fun!" *Potty Train Your Child in Just One Day* is based on proven toilet-training methods, cleverly incorporated into a theme party complete with treats, rewards, praise, encouragement, excitement, laughter, and lots of love, hugs, and kisses.

If you follow a few basic principles, temper tantrums, soiled clothes, and fears will quickly become a thing of the past. Rather than dwelling on what children do "wrong," the potty party focuses on what they do "right." The process is completed with lots of fanfare, very little stress, no tears, and preservation of both your and your child's self-esteem.

Modern marriages, dual careers, and time-sensitive schedules require new methods to achieve success. Loyal followers of Teri Crane, aptly naming her the "the Potty Pro," attest to her creative methods in achieving dry underwear. Many parents will agree this is no small achievement, but as Teri demonstrates, with proper preparation success is attainable in just one day. A student of psychology by training, a mother by experience, and an expert in potty training through necessity, Teri - has great ideas and the right credentials.

Potty Train Your Child in Just One Day is motivational, stimulating, and a lot of fun—with bits of humor throughout. I highly recommend this book.

Let the party begin!

Philip Caravella, M.D., F.A.A.F.P.
Department of Family Medicine,
The Cleveland Clinic Foundation

note to readers

I'd completely lost my bearings trying to follow potty-training instructions from a psychiatric expert. I was stuck on step one, which stated without an atom of irony: "Before you begin, remove all stubbornness from the child." . . . I knew it only could have been written by someone whose suit coat was still spotless at the end of the day, not someone who had any hands-on experience with an actual two-year-old.

—MARY KAY BLAKELY, journalist, mother, and
author of *American Mom: Motherhood, Politics, and Humble Pie*

Raising children brings countless rich and rewarding experiences into our lives. Potty training is typically not one of them.

If you're reading this book, it's probably not because you have an idle curiosity about toilet training or because you're planning ahead for the day when your own child will bid farewell to diapers. It's much more likely that you are a mom in potty-training hell, frantically searching for answers to ease the miserable time you and your child are having with this seemingly insurmountable hurdle.

If it's any consolation, you are not alone! In fact, you're in pretty good company. For many parents *and children,* toilet training is a power struggle filled with frustration, anxiety, and tears. I'm not proud to admit it, but that's exactly what happened when my son had to be toilet trained in order to be enrolled in preschool. In the heat of desperation, I bought a slew of potty-training books and read every one. Every book I read was too complicated, technical, or boring (sometimes all three). None of the books made toilet training easy, fun, or fast.

I tried every reasonable idea I read or heard, and some that were not reasonable—but nothing seemed to work. My inner critic mocked my every move, taunting me for losing yet another battle in what was fast becoming a potty-training war. Regardless of what I did, my son Spencer was completely content to continue wearing diapers and had absolutely no interest in using the toilet. I wondered if we would ever manage to cross this threshold. I had visions of Spencer going off to college, his backpack laden with books, calculator, pens, papers . . . and Pampers. Then again, if I couldn't get him potty-trained for preschool, he'd never make it to college!

As I pondered my dilemma, it occurred to me that Spencer didn't want to learn to use the potty because he had no real incentive to do so. The secret, I realized, was to make him an offer that he couldn't refuse. My bribe contained three simple, but magical words—Chuck E. Cheese! Basically, I told my son that we were going to have a potty-training party. If he potty trained the new doll I bought him and then used the potty himself, I would take him to Chuck E. Cheese to celebrate.

It worked! In just one day my son learned to use the toilet. And the best part was that we both enjoyed our time together that day. There were no angry words, no temper tantrums, and no tears!

Since that time, I have developed and refined the "One-Day Potty-Training Party" and taught this highly effective method to hundreds of other moms and dads in my Potty-Training Boot

Camp. I also do potty-training interventions when parents run into unexpected problems or encounter overwhelming resistance.

The One-Day Potty-Training Party is based on sound advice from experts, but I think it works so well because it's fun, easy, and rewarding for moms and kids. This fast, playful method raises children's self-esteem and leaves them bubbling with a sense of pride and accomplishment.

Moms who are fighting potty battles need straight answers fast, so I've made sure that *Potty Train Your Child in Just One Day* is a quick, easy read. It's divided into chapters that don't always go deep, but *do* go wide—we'll cover many topics and you'll get the information, guidance, charts, tips, checklists, and even the shopping lists you'll need to succeed.

For comic relief, the book is peppered with potty-training quotes and anecdotes from celebrities and everyday moms who have waged and won the potty war. You will also find creative tips from "Grandma," valuable insights from experts, and some fun potty facts and trivia. (Have you ever wondered how ancient Egyptian moms potty trained their kids?)

To make this process exciting and fun, I include a dozen detailed potty party themes, complete with suggestions for decorations, food and drinks, games, books, music, prizes, and presents. While all of these are fun, they are also critical in creating your own one-day potty-training event. To help you decide which theme party your child will find the most motivational and fun, I offer recommendations based on personality, preferences, and the concerns and fears your child has about using the potty.

Although the One-Day Potty-Training Party is endorsed by many physicians, it's still a good idea to discuss your plan of action with your child's pediatrician before you begin.

As you embark on this journey, be sure to listen to your own exquisitely sensitive parental intuition and pay close attention to what your child is feeling and saying about using the toilet. If he or she is truly not ready to be toilet trained, then nothing you do or say is going to work well. (I thoroughly cover the topic of readiness in chapter two.)

If your child *is* ready to be toilet trained, the One-Day Potty-Training Party is guaranteed to be simple, fun, rewarding, and very successful!

TERI CRANE, *The Potty Pro*

potty train your child in just one day

1. the secret's out— potty parties are in!

To every job that must be done, there is an element of fun.

—MARY POPPINS

Every day I'm besieged by telephone calls from moms who are confused, frustrated, and overwhelmed. Mostly they're at wit's end. They beg me for the secrets to potty training their children. And no matter what their particular potty woes might be, how long they've been trying to train their child, or how harrowing their bathroom battles, I invariably recommend a single, one-size-fits-all solution: Have a One-Day Potty-Training Party!

Kids love parties. In Toddler-Speak, a party means fun, games, cake, candy, presents, and prizes. For a two- or three-year-old, it doesn't get much better than that.

In Mom-Speak, a party can mean a fun way to motivate your child to learn a new behavior—in this case using the toilet. Giving your toddler motivation is critical to your success because when it comes to becoming toilet trained, most kids have absolutely no incentive. None. And when you look at it from their perspective, why would they? Life experience has proven that it's fast, easy, and convenient to go in their diapers.

No matter how much you want your child to trade in her Huggies for big-girl underpants, chances are she will remain blissfully unmotivated by your desire or concern. Plus, if a child has had a negative experience with the potty, it can be even more challenging to entice him to try it again.

According to the American Academy of Pediatrics, helping the 11 million children under the age of four through the potty-training process can be one of the toughest challenges for parents. Learning to use the potty is a key milestone in a child's development. Unlike other milestones associated with walking or talking, however, this developmental hurdle tends to be a source of considerable concern for both parent and child. A stressful potty-training period can damage a parent/child relationship and injure a child's self-esteem. But when this hurdle is successfully negotiated with a minimum of contention, it fosters a child's sense of independence and accomplishment.

DID YOU KNOW?

 From the time babies are born until they are toilet trained, they use an average of 4,000 diapers. $$$ Cha-Ching!

The One-Day Potty-Training Party is a fun, time-tested method for achieving potty-training victory. In the fast-paced, overscheduled, multitasking society in which we live, parents need a training tool that will teach them how to potty train their child in *one* day. The cost savings alone are enough incentive for most parents. And U.S. Census Bureau statistics indicate that American women are increasingly having more than two children. Even with our frantic schedules, we can attack this parenting challenge in an organized, structured fashion, with help from a tested routine. And as this book will demonstrate, that means a well-planned and exciting potty party!

There are a number of driving forces behind the push for quick and effective potty-training programs:

- Most preschools in the United States mandate that children cannot be promoted to the next level unless they are potty trained.

- Today, a mere 13 percent of America's families fit the 1950s model of husband as breadwinner and wife as homemaker. According to the U.S. Bureau of Labor Statistics, more than 60 percent of all marriages, 45 percent of the working population, are dual-career marriages. And nearly two-thirds of America's children attend some sort of out-of-home care on a regular basis.

- According to the *Children's Hospital Guide to Your Child's Health and Development,* 40 percent of three-year-olds still use diapers.

- Thirty-nine states and the District of Columbia spend a total of more than $1.9 billion a year on some sort of prekindergarten.

- The National Center for Health Statistics has reported that the number of women of childbearing age giving birth to three or more children rose 7 percent to 18.4 percent.

- A National Catalyst research survey found that more than 80 percent of new mothers return to the labor force within six months of childbirth.

I came up with the idea for a one-day potty-training party when I was desperate to toilet train my son Spencer so that he could be enrolled in preschool. Although at the time I felt like I was the only mother facing this challenge, I've since discovered that there are millions of moms in the same tight spot as I was in three years ago. According to the U.S. Census Bureau's Current Population Report, there are approximately 20 million parents with 11 million children under the age of four, and more than 4 million of those are currently enrolled in a nursery or preschool program where children often are not permitted to move up to the next level until they have been successfully potty trained. So even though the American Academy of Pediatrics suggests that there is no set age to begin potty training, the majority of preschool programs won't accept a three-year-old who isn't potty proficient.

EXPERTS SAY

Toilet training can be one of the most stressful experiences for children and their parents. Proper preparation and an organized, structured training approach are critical to success.

In a nutshell, the One-Day Potty-Training Party is based on solid toilet-training information and advice. But instead of a drawn out battle between parent and child, it's a one-day theme party where your child is the center of attention. Whatever theme you choose, the potty party is designed to be fast-paced, fun, and rewarding. Best of all, it works!

The Potty Party Has One Primary Goal

Make learning to use the potty fun by making the potty party one of the most exciting and rewarding days in your child's life.

GRANDMA SAYS

When you set out to teach a child something that she doesn't want to learn, a smooth landing often starts with a gentle push.

The Potty Party Is Divided into Three Parts

PART ONE

Give your child a new doll (preferably one that "wets") and the three of you have a party. While playing games, reading books, and watching potty-training videos, you teach the doll how to use the potty. Your child learns about the potty and how to use it by helping you teach his or her doll.

PART TWO

The theme party continues, but now the focus shifts to your child using the potty. Plenty of fun and rewards are built into this part of the party so that your child *wants* to use the potty and feels good about his or her success.

PART THREE

To celebrate your child's success, the party expands to include Dad, brothers and sisters, grandparents, and other close relations. Everyone congratulates your child for potty training his or her doll and for using the potty.

Since emerging from my own potty wars, I have gathered lots of knowledge and experience about potty training and throwing potty parties. By talking with child psychologists, parents, caregivers, professional party planners, and graduates of my Potty-Training Boot Camp, I have pulled together all the essential steps and vital ingredients to make a potty-training party a wonderful success. I include all the details and guidelines for planning and throwing the potty party in chapters five and six. But before you can begin planning the party and preparing your child for the big day, you need to determine whether he is physically and mentally ready for toilet training. And just as important, you need to determine whether *you* are ready! Don't even think about taking away your child's diapers before you take the readiness quiz in chapter two!

What Does It Mean to Be Potty Trained?

Everyone seems to have a different answer to this question. Rather than getting caught in the debate of who's right and who's wrong, I measure a child's potty-training success on a range from "not potty trained" to "totally potty trained."

CELEBRITY SCOOP

"The trick to potty training my boys Jamie and Bobby was to make a big deal out of it. I'd clap my hands and act really excited and tell them how smart and what big boys they were for making a poo-poo in the pot. That way they knew they did something really good."

—PAULA DEEN, CELEBRITY CHEF FROM THE FOOD NETWORK

When I launched my mission to toilet train my son, I asked (okay, *begged*) other moms to divulge their secrets to potty-training success. After a little probing, I often discovered that their child really wasn't potty trained at all, at least not by my understanding of the term. Basically, the child would go potty only if the mom undressed her, told her to sit on the potty, and waited, waited, waited, and waited a little more. Sometimes the child would go and sometimes she wouldn't. And as you might guess, accidents were part of the daily routine.

Well, call me crazy, but this version of toilet trained sounds more like a work in progress. Even so, it's important to remember that just getting a toddler to sit on the toilet and try can be a milestone on his path to being totally toilet trained.

Your toddler is totally potty trained when he can get in and out of the bathroom himself, get his pants down and back up

---

DID YOU KNOW?

Neanderthals designated toilet areas a short distance (and preferably downwind) from their caves, and they trained their children to use these areas.

---

again, clean his backside adequately, and wash his hands—all with minimal assistance. I have to tell you that when I first read this definition, it just increased my sense of frustration. I couldn't even get my son to *sit* on the potty. Getting him totally toilet trained seemed like an impossible dream. That's why it's important to celebrate every successful step. If your child can recognize that she has to use the bathroom—and tell you she needs to go in enough time for you to get her on the potty—that's a very successful step!

Waging the Potty War

Frankly, I was desperate. I'm not too proud to admit it. I was stressed out of my mind. The fact that toilet training is supposed to happen when our children are toddlers—at the height or on the heels of the Terrible Twos—seems like a cruel irony. At this age, getting a child to do anything she doesn't want to do can rapidly turn into a drama. So toilet training can be nothing short of traumatic. In our house, the potty battles escalated until we were engaged in what could only be called an all-out potty war! The fact that our son was winning made our efforts seem even more futile.

CELEBRITY SCOOP

"I figured if the kids are alive at the end of the day, I've done my job."

—ROSEANNE BARR

Here's what happened. When Spencer was about two and a half years old my husband, Kyle, and I bought him a potty-chair, set it in the bathroom, and told him (with enthusiasm) that he was a big boy now and it was time for him to learn to use the potty. And so began the first chapter of our potty-training saga. Nearly every day one of us would suggest to Spencer that he sit on the potty. Spencer's response was consistently "No!"

As his third birthday drew closer, he still adamantly refused to sit on his potty-chair and threw fits if we said the word "potty." But I persisted. When I picked him up from nursery school, I'd ask if he went on the potty "like a big boy." With a gleeful expression, he would inevitably tell me he went on the potty *every* time. His teachers, however, had an entirely different story: they said Spencer refused to even walk *near* the toilet. Worse, he'd frequently go off in a corner and poop in his big-boy underwear. His antipotty attitude was threatening to land him on the dreaded "Do Not Promote" list barring him graduation from nursery school to preschool.

Like most preschools in the United States, Spencer's had a rule that children could not enroll until they were potty trained. In other words: No potty, no preschool!

EXPERTS SAY

It is much more hygienic for children to use the potty than to wear diapers. Potty training your child is the most effective way to cure diaper rash, and it protects your child from long-term exposure to toxins in disposable diapers.

All of Spencer's successfully potty-trained friends were going to be promoted to preschool and he was about to be left behind—all because he couldn't go to the bathroom by himself. That's when I went from being frustrated to being paranoid.

I started thinking everyone was in on the joke but me. I

mean, why couldn't I figure this thing out? Was the secret of potty training only revealed to those who knew a special password or handshake? Was that why some moms boasted that their children practically potty trained themselves, while the rest of us struggled to solve the mystery? I became obsessed and utterly desperate to enter the inner sanctum of potty-training success.

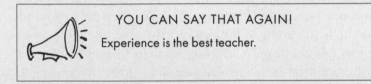

YOU CAN SAY THAT AGAIN!
Experience is the best teacher.

Meanwhile, the battle persisted and my son and I were both miserable. I no longer wanted to keep teaching him and he no longer wanted to try to learn. Resigned and feeling like a failure, I decided to put the whole project on hold for a while. My husband and I made a pact that we would do absolutely nothing to encourage Spencer to use the toilet–no more discussions, no more pleading or bribing, and, God help us, no more tears!

The potty-chair went into the closet; the big-boy underwear and training pants went back in the drawer from which they came. I told myself that surely Spencer would decide on his own–at some point–that he didn't want to wear diapers anymore, and I bit my tongue waiting for that day to arrive. (At the very least, I consoled myself, he'd definitely be motivated by the time he started dating.)

Each day I eagerly watched my son for signs that he no longer wanted to wear a diaper. But not another word about using the potty was mentioned.

Until, that is, I turned the calendar page and was reminded that Spencer's preschool deadline was just around the bend. With a renewed determination to beat the clock, I devoured all the toilet-training material I could find. I read books, watched videos, and perused websites. I picked the brain of every mother I encountered who had something valuable to share about the fastest route to potty-training victory. I also talked to scores of moms who were feeling just as confused and frustrated about potty training as I was.

As the deadline for preschool enrollment loomed, I became more and more desperate. My husband had great intentions, but he was actually hindering the process. Like a lot of dads, he was taking an authoritarian tone with our son, subtly *demanding* that he begin going to the potty by himself, like a big boy. I knew enough about potty training by then to realize that the authoritarian approach was doomed to backfire. According to everything I learned from experts and other moms, kids typically dig in their heels when adults make demands about potty training, and pressure makes them actively hostile.

To make matters worse, Spencer was now just one week away from his third birthday. I silently concluded that if I could teach him *before* he turned three, I could truthfully tell anyone who asked that he was potty trained when he was "only" two. I needed a shortcut. The time for drastic action was at hand!

DID YOU KNOW?

Disposable diapers are the third biggest contributor to landfills.

Necessity Is the Mother of Invention

I had read that one of the ways parents could teach a toddler to use the potty was to first guide the toddler to teach a doll to use the potty. The question was, how could I get my son to do this in a way that would be fun for both of us? I had already tried giving him candy and other bribes, so I knew I had to come up with an incentive that he would think was awesome. And then it occurred to me like a flash of lightning: a party! All I had to do was say the word "party" and Spencer's eyes would light up. I would plan an all day party for the specific purpose of potty training my son!

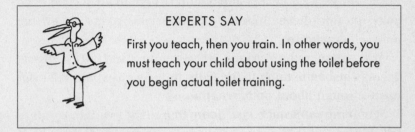

EXPERTS SAY

First you teach, then you train. In other words, you must teach your child about using the toilet before you begin actual toilet training.

Our potty party began at 9 A.M. Saturday morning when I handed Spencer a wrapped present. Spencer thought it was fantastic that he got a present on a day that wasn't his birthday or a holiday. The present was a doll that he and I would potty train together. He quickly bonded with the doll and named him "Dolly," and he happily bought into the plan that he and I were going to teach Dolly to use the potty. All morning, in between reading books and playing games, I taught Dolly how a big boy goes to the potty by himself and Spencer watched closely. By lunchtime, Spencer had grasped the most important aspects of potty training and was teaching Dolly by himself.

GRANDMA SAYS

Monkey see, monkey do. Your children may not do what you say, but they will do what you do.

After lunch, for added incentive, I told Spencer that if he showed me that he could use the potty like a big boy—just like Dolly—we would call up Grandma and Granddad and all go to Chuck E. Cheese to celebrate. Chuck E. Cheese was the most enticing carrot I could dangle in front of Spencer. He was crazy for the place! I used to have to drive several miles out of my way to the grocery store to dodge the Chuck E. Cheese landmarks my son recognized, or he would pitch a royal fit!

As it turned out, playing the Chuck E. Cheese card worked like a charm. By 5 P.M. Spencer could tell when he needed to go potty, go into the bathroom, pull down his pants, sit on the potty-chair, and go.

And guess what? When we went to Chuck E. Cheese, Spencer used the toilet there with no problem at all. We even made a potty pit stop on the way home.

When my husband came home that night I couldn't wait to tell him what happened. Kyle was happy, but thought it sounded too good to be true. Considering what the past six months had been like, I couldn't blame him for doubting. Spencer had used the potty six or seven times throughout the day, but I silently worried that the magic might wear off. And so it was with mixed emotions that I left Spencer with Kyle that evening and headed out for a friend's baby shower.

Much to my relief and delight, around 8 P.M. Kyle called my cell phone and exclaimed, "Spencer went to the bathroom by himself!" Success—you are sweet, indeed!

It's Not a Shortcut If You Get Lost

The One-Day Potty-Training Party is a fun and very effective process if you properly prepare for the big day and follow all of the steps in the correct order.

If you attempt to do this program without following the steps in the order they are presented, your child will *not* be potty trained in *one* day. It's as simple as that.

I have tested all the steps and worked with hundreds of parents to determine which ones are critical to success and which are helpful but not necessary. If you follow the steps in the sequence I have outlined you'll be amazed at the wonderful results. I promise.

For those of you who are already contemplating ways to make this shortcut even shorter, I beg you to slow down and take a few deep breaths. The more desperately you want your child potty trained *now*, the more you need to back off and adopt a less urgent approach. The One-Day Potty-Training Party won't be a shortcut if you get lost along the way or hit a roadblock because you didn't properly prepare your child or yourself.

Please don't flip through this book and think you have it mastered. Parents who have tried an à la carte version of this method—choosing to do some steps and skipping or racing through others—invariably hit a dead end. And nobody wants that.

Like learning to walk, your child needs to take one step at a time. Do not encourage your child to jump to the next step until he masters the one he is on. Each step builds on the previous one—and the order is very important.

GRANDMA SAYS

If you want your child to be a quick study, give her straight A's: Acceptance, Approval, Appreciation, Admiration, and Applause.

Some of the steps may seem obvious or overly simplistic. But when they are used in combination with the rest of the program, they create a profound physical and emotional change while making learning fun. By allowing your child enough time to practice and become comfortable and proficient with each step, you help build her self-confidence. Each step can be celebrated as a milestone in your child's progress toward potty proficiency.

> ## TRAIN ONE TWIN
> ## (TRIPLET, QUADRUPLET, QUINTUPLET, ETC.) AT A TIME!
>
> Over the past twenty years, the number of multiple births in the United States has increased more than 70 percent. So lots of parents ask me whether to potty train their kids at the same time. My answer is almost always no. The potty party is designed as a one-on-one experience and won't be as effective if you are training more than one child at a time. Plus, although you may be ready for all your toddlers to be potty trained, chances are they will not all be ready at the same time, even if they are identical siblings. I recommend that you train your children in the order of their readiness. Those who are trained first can become cheerleaders for their brothers and sisters.

The majority of parents I work with potty train their child within a twenty-four-hour period, and the average time for complete training is around four to six hours. Some children were trained in one hour and others took up to two days. Even the fastest learners will need consistent reinforcement in the days and weeks following the potty party until it becomes a natural part of their day.

That's not to say there aren't special cases that need special tactics. Later in the book, we'll discuss how to potty train children with special needs, including children who have limited verbal skills and those who are prone to tantrums. We'll also cover how to help children who have continuous accidents and how to motivate toddlers who simply prefer diapers to big-kid underwear. Some of these challenges are more daunting than others, but they are all solvable with the right knowledge, preparation, and mindset.

2. ready or not— timing is everything!

For everything there is a season,
and a time for every purpose under heaven.

–ECCLESIASTES 3:1

Toilet training can be fraught with tears, promises, threats, and enough bribery to make Tony Soprano look like the good guy! Fortunately, it doesn't have to be that way. But it *will* be that way–I guarantee it–*if your child is not ready to be toilet trained.*

Trying to potty train a child before he is physically, mentally, and emotionally ready is like trying to teach a newborn to stand on his own two feet. Before an infant can stand up, his body has to reach a certain stage of development. No one gets angry with a newborn for not being able to stand on his own, but many parents become upset with toddlers who are not responding to toilet training. According to a 1994 article in *Your Health*, toilet-training accidents are the leading catalyst of serious abuse of children over age one. Obviously, a lot of parents need to be better informed and much more prepared to take on this task. It is also not uncommon for a toddler who is ready for toilet training to have a mom, dad, or both who are not ready.

The moms in my Potty-Training Boot Camp often admit that

DID YOU KNOW?

A child must understand the link between needing to eliminate and actually doing it before she can be successfully potty trained.

they started trying to potty train their kids sooner than they thought they should. Why? Pressure! Lots of well-meaning parents just can't seem to stop themselves from comparing their child's progress and development with that of other children. When I was entrenched in a potty war with my son, nothing got my blood pressure skyrocketing quicker than the question "So, how's potty training going?" My mommy shields would instantly go up. *What* exactly *does she mean by* going? *Does she mean, "Have you started?" or "Are you finished?"*

Rather than tell a barefaced lie, I'd just smile and nonchalantly flip the zinger back into her court with a question like "So, is little Janie potty training *too?*" *Too* was the operative word. When it worked, I sighed with relief to have headed off yet another round in the ongoing My Kid's Better Than Your Kid Competition.

Since potty training is one of the first major hurdles that moms have to teach children to jump, it is a very important step in earning our Mommy Merit Badge. As all mothers with toddlers discover, this is a universal, yet unspoken truth. If we get through the experience relatively unscathed, or at least with no permanent facial ticks, we can silently conclude we are good mothers. So, try not to cave in to the pressure of competition—don't set off on the toilet-training trail until you're sure that you and your child are both ready!

Changing Traditions

For the past several decades, the right age to begin potty training has been increasing, particularly in North America. In the 1930s, most mothers started training their babies when they were around three months old. In 1946, Dr. Benjamin Spock advised mothers to wait until their infants were between seven and nine months old. In the early 1960s, T. Berry Brazelton, pediatrician and best-selling author, said parents should wait until children were between two and two and a half years old before beginning potty training. At that time, 90 percent of toddlers under the age of two were not yet potty trained.

By the mid- to late 1980s, close to 50 percent of parents were waiting until their child's second birthday before they began toilet training. Then, in 1999, Dr. Brazelton revised his earlier recommendation of beginning when a child is two and said that children would not be ready for training until after age three. His recommendations were officially adopted by the American Academy of Pediatrics, and today, one-third of children still wear diapers after their third birthday.

DID YOU KNOW?

At around twenty-four months, children begin learning how to solve problems by picturing a solution and planning a way to accomplish it. Once a child can actively solve problems—like how can I get my favorite doll back from my brother, or how can I get Mommy to let me stay up later—she is cognitively ready to begin toilet training.

It's interesting to note that the right potty training age also differs from one culture and geographic region to another, even if they are close in distance. For instance, in the mid-1960s, children in London were starting their potty training before

TOP 10 POTTY-TRAINING READINESS MYTHS

YOUR CHILD IS READY TO BE POTTY TRAINED WHEN:

10. She can say the word "potty."

9. He sees big kid superhero underpants on TV and begs you to buy them.

8. You find out you're the only mom on the street who has a three-year-old who isn't potty trained yet.

7. She discovers the joy of flushing innocent objects—toys, money, your new lipstick—down the toilet.

6. He delights in shouting new words like "penis" while you're in crowded department stores.

5. You find out that "diaper-wearing toddlers" are banned from your local preschool.

4. She asks her Sunday school teacher, "Sister Maria, do you have a vagina too?"

3. He pees on the fire hydrant—following the example of his dog.

2. Your fantasies of chocolate, romance, and passion are suddenly overrun by wistful thoughts of a diaper-free day.

1. Your husband proudly proclaims that his mother had him toilet trained before he was two years old and suggests that you give "Mumsy" a call.

they were five months old, while Parisian children—just across the English Channel—weren't starting until they were almost eight months old. Just to the north in Stockholm, potty training usually began a few weeks after the child's first birthday.

Since most kids can barely walk at twelve months, the meaning of "potty trained" in the 1965 study fell decidedly short of *our* definition for totally potty trained. In the study, children were considered potty trained if they could tell their moms they had to go potty soon enough for their moms to rush them to the bathroom, pull down their pants, and hold them over the potty. As I said in chapter one, that *is* worth celebrating—but it isn't the end result that you're striving for.

My grandmother Nana, who came from Ireland in the early 1900s, once told me it was very common for parents to "catch" an infant's waste in a small pot, or better yet, to hold them over a patch of grass instead of using a nappy. She said parents in America were still using the grass patch technique until the early 1940s. Can you imagine grabbing your youngster (just as he's about to do the pee-pee dance on your carpet) and running outside for a patch of grass? YIKES! Hooray for disposables!

Meanwhile, in a 1977 study, anthropologists found evidence of numerous successful potty-training methods among supposedly primitive East African tribes. It may surprise you that these parents appear to be far more sophisticated than their Western counterparts when it comes to listening for cues to their kids' readiness. The parents in these tribes begin potty training with a soothing, calm approach shortly after birth, and they are able to achieve day and night dryness by the age of five or six months! These kids are not undressing and dressing themselves and they're not using toilets in the sense that we think of them, but they *are* able to tell when they need to go to the bathroom and take care of it themselves. Might there be an important lesson for us?

CELEBRITY SCOOP

"In the final analysis, it is not what you do for your children but what you have taught them to do for themselves that will make them successful human beings."

—ANN LANDERS

How Old Should My Child Be for Potty Training?

Although there is no standard age for when toilet training should begin for all children, many toddlers are ready when they are between two and a half and three years old. The trend used to be to get them started sooner, but now many moms are waiting until their kids are nearing their third birthday or even longer. However, the trend to begin sooner rather than later still seems to be strong in large cities such as New York and Los Angeles.

There is no clear agreement on when a child's nervous system is fully able to transmit the signals associated with a full

DID YOU KNOW?

There is no relation between the age a child is toilet trained and his level of intelligence.

bowel and bladder. However, the general consensus of the medical community is that a child cannot master complete voluntary control until she is at least eighteen months old.

As a child grows, the nerve connections continue to develop until about age thirteen. A grade-school student has many neural connections developing to the bladder and bowel, but not as many as an adult. This explains why younger children may occasionally wet their pants, while older children and teenagers very seldom do.

EXPERTS SAY

When you first begin potty training, your child's ability to recognize the sensations that mean "I have to pee" or "I have to poop" is not fully developed. This awareness develops *during* the potty-training process.

YOU CAN SAY THAT AGAIN!

"The most important thing that parents can teach their children is how to get along without them."

—FRANK A. CLARK, AUTHOR

In her nationally syndicated column, Dr. Sylvia Rimm, who directs the Family Achievement Clinic at The Cleveland Clinic Foundation and is a clinical professor of psychiatry and pediatrics at Case School of Medicine, said, "A few generations ago, it was typical to train babies quite a bit earlier than we do today. However, the parents were actually more trained than the babies. In other words, if parents put their baby on the potty regularly at fifteen months or so, she might achieve success, but she would not yet be ready to let a parent know when she needed to go potty. By age two, the parent still needs to take charge of initiating the potty training, but many toddlers are able to understand and report their need to go potty."

FROM THE MOUTHS OF BABES

When I was potty training my son, Ken, I told him that if he had to urinate and wanted to tell me, he could call it number one in front of other people. If he had to have a bowel movement, he could tell me that he had to go number two. He readily took to this code and thought it was fun that he and I had a little secret.

A few weeks later we were attending our church carnival and Ken and I were watching people bet on the roulette wheel. The young man standing next to us had placed his chip on number two to win a large stuffed panda bear. When the wheel was given a spin, the man shouted, "Gimme a number two. I need a number two!" Ken turned to me and said, "That guy must really gotta go!"

When Is Your Child Ready for a Potty Party?

A number of child psychologists report that it's emotionally and psychologically beneficial for moms to wait until children are around three years old to begin potty training. I agree with them, but I often wonder if we'd be willing to wait this long if we didn't have disposable diapers! Those little buggers are both a blessing and a curse. I have found that readiness varies for every child, and age is often less of a factor than desire.

Most of today's moms shudder at the thought of going back to cloth diapers. Even if we've never used one, we've heard the diaper rash horror stories and we can easily imagine the inconvenience of washing them, not to mention the nose-pinching odor! The catch-22 is that your child is more likely to grasp the connection between cause and effect—going and feeling wet or soiled—if she's wearing a cloth diaper or cloth training pants.

POTTY-TRAINING BOOT CAMP TIP

 If it doesn't look clean and smell clean, it's not clean. Chlorine bleach won't remove the urine odor from clothing and sheets. To make them smell fresh, soak them in an enzyme bleach or borax solution before washing them. (Potty-training veterans also recommend commercial products like Bac-Out Stain & Odor Remover with live enzyme cultures.)

In my desperate need to potty train my son Spencer so that he could enter preschool, I threw myself on the grenade and decided to use cloth diapers—but only when we were at home. (I was determined to succeed, but I'm not a saint or a martyr!) I made this decision after waiting several months for Spencer to tell me he was ready to try potty training again. One day turned into the next and my son remained content with his carefree Pampers lifestyle.

Finally I came to a stunning conclusion. If I waited for Spencer to tell me he was ready, I would wait forever! Or at least a lot longer than I knew I could wait. The consensus of

---

DID YOU KNOW?

Children between the ages of two and three take great pleasure in their own accomplishments, and they are enthusiastic about improving their abilities and skills.

EXPERTS SAY

When a child is about three years old, he begins to become aware of social identity and wants to be able to do what the other kids his age are doing. If he is not yet toilet trained, just knowing that his friends are all wearing big boy pants and using the potty can motivate him to join them.

more than a hundred moms is that waiting for a toddler to say, "I want to use the potty," is like waiting for a teenager to say, "I want to clean my room." It's reportedly happened a few times, but no one should expect it. So, after determining that Spencer was, in fact, physically and emotionally ready, I proceeded confidently with my potty-training party plan.

Signs of Readiness

My wonderful family physician and consultant for this book, Dr. Philip Caravella of The Cleveland Clinic Foundation, reports that developing bowel and bladder control is a skill a child needs to master in order to conquer the intricacies of the toilet. Along with understanding bodily sensations, they must learn when to head for the bathroom and how to remove their clothes, sit on the potty, and relax their sphincter muscles in order to eliminate. Pretty tall order for these little people, wouldn't you say?

Most experts agree that potty-training readiness typi-

DAYTIME BOWEL CONTROL

Physical signs that indicate readiness for daytime bowel control include

- Regular pattern of bowel movements
- Complete nighttime bowel control
- Pausing while playing to have a BM
- Making grunting noises or getting red in the face or even crying as she learns to relax and contract her sphincter muscle to push her BMs out

These outward signs show that her business is becoming more voluntary and that she is becoming more aware.

cally follows a sequence, with bowel control usually coming before bladder control. The typical readiness sequence is:

1. Nighttime bowel control
2. Daytime bowel control
3. Daytime bladder control
4. Nighttime bladder control

Take the following quiz to assess your child's readiness.

Potty-Training Readiness Quiz ★ ★ ★ ★ ★ ★

1. Does your child relate to and imitate older children?
2. Can your child safely walk to and away from the toilet?
3. Is your child starting to understand where her toys and other possessions belong?
4. Is the number of times your child says no or responds negatively decreasing?
5. Is your child interested in trying to do things "by himself"?
6. Does your child know that some of her peers are successfully using the potty?
7. Can your child understand what you mean by "using the potty" and "no more diapers," and can he talk about this topic with you?
8. Is your child's diaper staying dry longer?
9. Does your child frequently wake up with a dry diaper?
10. Is your child stopping play to squat for a bowel movement?

Scoring Recommendations:
Each yes is worth one point.

SCORE: ☆ ☆ ☆ ☆ ☆
8–10 Your child is probably ready to begin potty training.
5–7 Wait a month or so and take the quiz again.
1–4 Wait a few months and take the quiz again.

Are You Ready, Willing, and Able?

I think Dr. Spock, whose advice helped raise most of America's baby boomers, had it right a half century ago. In his trailblazing book, *The Common Sense Book of Baby and Child Care* (for years, this book ranked second in all-time sales behind only the Bible), "Everyone talks about the child's readiness to be trained, but parents have to be ready too. Many feel anxious about the whole business."

The anxiety to successfully potty train your child can come from any number of sources. It could be from your peers—a result of that sometimes subtle, sometimes obvious, but always competitive race that unfortunately many parents run, pushing their kids toward each developmental mile marker.

Pressure can also come from your parents or your in-laws. Are you among the unfortunates who are sensing the silent reproach that you're failing as a mom because your three-year-old is still in diapers? Well, relax. Despite what your mother or mother-in-law might say, your child will not suffer for it later in life. For lots of moms, the pressure is self-inflicted. If you have a type-A personality and you've declared a potty-training deadline, I'm sorry to be the one to

---

BLADDER CONTROL

Physical signs that indicate readiness for bladder control include

- A dry diaper for more than a few hours
- An increasing number of dry diapers after naptime
- An increasing number of dry diapers in the morning

These periods of dryness are examples that the bladder is growing and able to hold urine for greater periods of time. It also shows that your child's awareness level is growing along with his physical maturity.

Signs that show your child understands she has urinated or had a BM:

- Asking you to change his diaper if it is wet or soiled
- Pulling or tugging at her diaper, trying to pull it off herself
- Crying, fussing, or simply proclaiming "poopy" while pointing to his diaper

All these outward reactions demonstrate that the child understands he has urinated or had a BM.

DON'T BEGIN POTTY TRAINING WHEN

- **You have recently moved into a new home.** Give your child at least a few months to adjust to the new environment.

- **You are going to or have just recently expanded your family.** This includes giving birth, adopting, and blending families through marriage. Your toddler will need lots of positive attention during this transition, and learning new skills can be too challenging if he feels stress about the change. He may even revert to baby behaviors that he gave up a while back, such as sucking his thumb, wanting a bottle, or using "baby talk."

- **You are going through or have just gone through a major "family loss."** This could include separating from or divorcing your partner or another loss such as the death of a family member, pet, or close relative.

- **You have recently changed child-care providers or preschool teachers.** One big change at a time is more than enough for a young child. Wait until you see her comfort level increase with the new teacher or situation before embarking on toilet training.

tell you, but there's a good chance that the pressure you're feeling will only make matters worse. From time to time all moms worry that the kids are not growing, learning, or progressing fast enough. There's an underlying concern that if she's not "on track" there may be something wrong with her or with us! When you're feeling like this, or feeling the pressure of family and peers, make a mental note to recall the following example of one of the world's all-time greatest geniuses:

By some accounts, Albert Einstein did not say a word until well past his third birthday. According to the story, his first words were not "mama" or "dada" as you might imagine, but "This soup is hot!" His astonished parents, who had been worried that something was wrong with their son, asked him why he waited so long to talk. "Because," Einstein report-

---

CELEBRITY SCOOP

"You know the only people who are always sure about the proper way to raise children? Those who've never had any."

—BILL COSBY

edly said, "up until now every-thing was fine."

Peer pressure and personal anxieties aside, for many moms, the desperation to potty train comes in a far more tangible form. Most preschool programs won't accept a child for enrollment or allow him to progress to the next level along with his friends unless he has emerged like a fluttering butterfly from the smelly cocoon of his diapers. Most preschools start in September and have strict no-diaper rules. If your child is slated for preschool enrollment but isn't diaper-free by the starting date, he or she will have to wait another year to attend. So you need help.

Way back in the less-complicated 1950s, Dr. Spock noted that parents need as much support for their anxieties over potty training as their kids. In fact, if you read between the lines of *Baby and*

REMEMBER THIS...

- Thomas Edison's teachers said he was too stupid to learn anything.

- Walt Disney was fired by a newspaper editor for lack of ideas. He also went bankrupt several times before he built Disneyland.

- Louisa May Alcott, the author of *Little Women*, was discouraged to write. Instead she was told by her family to find work as a servant or seamstress.

- One of Albert Einstein's teachers described him as "mentally slow, unsociable and adrift forever in his foolish dreams." He was also expelled and refused admittance to the Zurich Polytechnic School.

- Beethoven handled the violin poorly and preferred playing his own compositions instead of improving his technique. His teacher called him hopeless as a composer.

- An expert said of Vince Lombardi (most winning percentage coach in football history): "He possesses minimal football knowledge and lacks motivation."

- After Fred Astaire's first screen test, the memo from the testing director of MGM read, "Can't act! Slightly bald! Can dance a little!" Astaire kept the framed memo over the fireplace in his Beverly Hills home.

GRANDMA SAYS

You attract more flies with honey than vinegar. The more you praise your child for doing right, the less he'll do wrong.

EXPERTS SAY

According to the American Academy of Pediatrics, moms who started training their toddlers at
age two had them trained by the time they turned
three. Moms who started potty training at eighteen months or younger did not have their children
potty trained until after they turned four.

Child Care, I think he was implying that when it comes to potty training, the parent–not the toddler–is the tougher nut to crack. My observation and experience with moms who are potty training is that when they've resolved their own anxieties over this issue, their children feel more relaxed and less anxious, and they are therefore more able to understand and practice this new skill.

It's important to keep in mind that Dr. Spock made this observation when few Americans had a television in their home, much less all the contemporary electronic distractions such as video games, cell phones, and the Internet. He was speaking at a time when American kids spent hour after hour of unstructured time simply *playing,* rather than being chauffeured about by parents on an endless loop of music lessons, sporting events, and structured play dates. And in that world, one of the parents was likely home with the children all day.

You don't need me to tell you that that world no longer exists, at least for the vast majority of us. And with our considerably quicker pace, is it really surprising to suggest that as overscheduled, multitasking, double-career American parents, we might be a tad too haphazard in our parenting habits for our children to learn to go to the bathroom like adults, on our schedule, in our prescribed fashion? Often we're so busy that we unwittingly ignore our child's own cues altogether, which can prolong the potty-training phase from months to even years.

The potty-training phase goes most quickly when children can learn in a fun, positive atmosphere. Parents who use an authoritarian or disciplinary teaching approach with a child will most likely prolong the training phase. So if you see potty training as a disciplinary concern, it is important to begin to look at it from a different perspective. After all, when your baby was learning to walk, you didn't punish him when he fell down, and the same principle should apply for potty training. Toddlers don't fall down to deliberately disobey their parents and they don't have accidents in their pants to make a statement. Falling down and having bladder and bowel control accidents are simply part of growing up.

With that said, some moms—although they may not want to admit it—find potty training so tedious and frustrating that they can't do it without becoming upset. I know how easy it is to feel stressed out, exhausted, and overwhelmed by the whole process! Still, if it's producing so much anxiety for you that you're frequently feeling angry, give yourself the freedom and power to recruit a Potty-Training Pinch Hitter. The fact is, as moms, we excel in some areas and struggle in others. For your sake and the sake of your child, you need to be totally honest with yourself as to whether you are the best person to host your child's potty-training party.

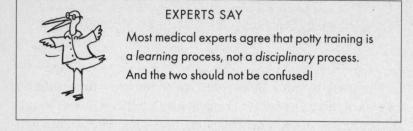

EXPERTS SAY

Most medical experts agree that potty training is a *learning* process, not a *disciplinary* process. And the two should not be confused!

If the idea of spending an entire day teaching, coaching, motivating, encouraging, and basically being your child's potty-training cheerleader makes you feel like you'll need a straitjacket and a bottle of tranquilizers, start making a list of potential pinch hitters. Your pinch hitter can be your spouse or a grandparent or other relative, friend, or neighbor. There's no shame in delegating this important job to someone else. There *is* shame in damaging your child's self-esteem by punishing her or getting angry with her for being a normally developing child who is struggling to learn something new.

For The One-Day Potty-Training Party to work, the party host and the child have to have fun and the host has to stick to the structure of the program. The host needs to dispense plenty of praise, hugs, and positive reinforcement. Knowing yourself is as important as knowing your child if you want to have a positive, tearless training experience. (And who doesn't!)

Potty-Training Party Coach Quiz ★★★★★

Take this quiz to see whether you're ready, willing, and able to assume the role of Potty-Training Party Coach.

1. I lose my temper quickly.

NEVER   RARELY   SOMETIMES   OFTEN

2. I am very goal oriented and get frustrated when I feel like I'm behind schedule.

NEVER   RARELY   SOMETIMES   OFTEN

3. When my child misbehaves, spills something, or upsets me, I say or do things that I regret.

NEVER   RARELY   SOMETIMES   OFTEN

4. When my child doesn't listen, I raise my voice and yell.

NEVER   RARELY   SOMETIMES   OFTEN

5. My emotions, rather than my child's actions, tend to determine the severity of punishment that I choose.

NEVER   RARELY   SOMETIMES   OFTEN

6. In the course of one day, I will lose my patience with my child.

NEVER   RARELY   SOMETIMES   OFTEN

SCORING:

NEVER = 0   RARELY = 1   SOMETIMES = 2   OFTEN = 3

Add up all your points:

0–3   Wow! You are either kidding yourself, or you're up for Parent of the Year! Keep up the great work and have a blast at your child's potty party.

4–8   You keep your emotions in fairly good balance. If you're excited about being your child's Potty-Training Party Coach and you can be well rested going into the party day, you can do a great job!

9–13   It sounds like you're dealing with a moderate to high level of stress and tension. Until or unless you can truly calm down, increase your patience, and lower your expectations, you may want to consider enlisting the help of a Potty-Training Pinch Hitter.

14–18 Yikes! You need an immediate vacation. Your short fuse can have a very negative effect on your child, so it's crucial that you take steps to lower your stress level and learn how to be more patient, positive, and pleasant. Start making a list of potential Potty-Training Pinch Hitters, and have your prospects take this quiz before you honor anyone with the job!

GRANDMA SAYS

You can't make a child do better by making her feel worse.

During the Potty-Training Party and throughout the maintenance phase, there is absolutely no spanking, punishing, scolding, or disapproving comments. Verbal abuse can be as damaging as physical abuse to a child's psyche. It's imperative for a child to have a strong sense of confidence and self-esteem in order to learn new developmental skills. How much fun would you have if you were at a party and the host was criticizing and reprimanding you? Probably not a lot. When a parent ridicules or hurts a child's feelings during potty training, they both take several steps back, thus prolonging the training phase. A potty party can—and should—be exciting. And it is this excitement, coupled with your child's own natural energy and the adult host's positive attitude, that will make for a memorable and successful event.

3. welcome to potty world! making the best choices for your child

Child rearing myth number 1: Labor ends when the baby is born.

One of the secrets to potty-training success is making sure you have all the essential equipment and supplies *before* you begin. If your child is displaying some of the readiness signs discussed in the last chapter, it's not too early to do a little preparatory shopping.

In chapter six, Potty Party Plans and Themes, I've listed books, videos, games, snacks, drinks, and all sorts of potty-training paraphernalia that will make the party more fun and more successful. To make your life a little easier, I've even included shopping lists for each theme party. But for now, let's just focus on the potty-training essentials.

Potty-Training Essentials

Potty-chair that is easily emptied
or potty seat adapter with footstool (most moms prefer
potty-chairs)

Baby doll (preferably one that wets)

Doll's underwear

Training pants

Disposable pull-ups

Big-kid underwear
   (one size bigger than your child would normally wear)

Potty chart (preferably two)

Flushable wet wipes

Waterproof mattress covers (preferably two)

Waterproof blanket

YOU CAN SAY THAT AGAIN!

"We worry about what a child will be tomorrow, yet we forget that he is someone today."

—STACIA TAUSCHER

Potty-Chairs

There are three secrets to selecting the best potty-chair for your child. The first is safety, the second is size, and the third is simplicity. In other words, the potty-chair must be stable and pass all safety ratings. Your toddler's bottom must fit comfortably on the seat. And the potty must be simple to use and easy to clean. If you live in a large house or apartment or have two stories, consider buying more than one potty-chair. Expecting a potty novice to make it from one end of the house to the other or up or down a flight of stairs in time is probably asking too much.

Whether or not to involve your child in the process of selecting and buying a potty-chair is best determined by your observation and instincts. If your child has been showing interest in the toilet and wants to do practically everything "by myself!" then bringing her along to select a potty is probably a good idea.

On the other hand, if your child seems reluctant or afraid of the toilet or has already expressed disinterest in using a potty, then choose one you think he'll like and hide it until the day of your potty-training party.

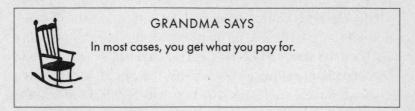

GRANDMA SAYS

In most cases, you get what you pay for.

SAFETY FIRST

Most potty-chairs look innocent enough and all chairs sold in the United States must pass safety ratings. But some are safer than others. When you shop for a potty-chair, consider the following safety questions:

1. Can this chair be rocked or tipped?
2. Can my child slide or fall off the side or back of this chair?
3. Are there any sharp, pointed, or protruding pieces that can scrape, scratch, puncture, or bump my child?
4. Are there any parts that can move, slide, or pinch my child?

The answer to all four questions should obviously be no!

DID YOU KNOW?

The oldest working flushing toilet is in Greece. This 4,000-year-old relic was way ahead of its time!

ONE SIZE DOESN'T FIT ALL

Where potty-chairs are concerned, size matters! If your toddler's bottom is draping over the seat or barely covering the inside rim, she'll probably feel uncomfortable, anxious, or both.

If the chair fits your toddler well, he will be able to sit down on it with no assistance, his bottom will rest comfortably and solidly on the seat, and his feet will reach the floor. If your child is excited about getting her own potty, then by all means bring her along for the shopping. The best way to tell if the seat fits your child is to have her sit on it. However, if your child is reluctant to use a potty, you can buy the right size by measuring him ahead of time.

HOW TO MEASURE FOR GOOD FIT

To buy the correct height:

1. Measure from the back of your child's knees to the floor.
2. Measure the potty-chair from the seat to the floor.

To buy the right size seat:

1. Have your child sit on a large piece of clean paper and, using a pen or felt tip marker, trace from the outside top of his right thigh, around his bottom, and to the top of his left thigh.
2. Cut out the "bottom pattern," fold it up, and take it with you to the store.

As you examine each chair, consider the following questions:

1. Will my child's bottom fit comfortably on this seat?
2. Can my child sit on the potty-chair with her feet flat on the floor?

3. Will this potty-chair fit into my child's bathroom?

4. Will this potty-chair fit into my car? (Only a concern if you plan to take it with you to friends' or relatives' homes.)

POTTY-TRAINING BOOT CAMP TIP

Portable camping toilets can make great potty-training chairs for children who are bigger or heavier than their peers.

KEEP IT SIMPLE

Just like any other appliance or piece of equipment, the more moving parts, gadgets, and frills, the higher the price and the greater the chance of pieces breaking or becoming damaged. Simplicity also refers to how easy it is for you to empty and clean the potty. And I say, the easier the better!

CELEBRITY SCOOP

"I see myself as a coach getting my children to the play-off, which is life. It's like sending a rocket to the moon: You may lose contact, but if you programmed it right, it will come back home."

—DAMON WAYANS

Although some parents favor potty-chairs with trays, I recommend using the trays with care and caution. Under no circumstances should you ever use the tray to keep your child confined to the potty-chair. If your toddler feels trapped, he may hurt his fingers by trying to remove the tray. Perhaps worse is the fear and anxiety that being confined can create. If a child has a frightening or frustrating experience with toilet training, she's likely to slam on the potty-training brakes and refuse to go anywhere near her potty-chair.

You can rate a potty-chair's simplicity by asking the following questions:

1. Is the potty-chair made of smooth, sturdy plastic?
2. Is there a removable toilet bowl or cup that I can easily slide out to empty and clean?
3. If the potty-chair has moving parts or gadgets, are they safely secured and easy to clean?
4. If the potty-chair has a safety shield, is it easy to remove and reattach?

CELEBRITY SCOOP

"The arrival of a baby coincides with the departure of our minds. My wife and I often summoned the grandparents of our first baby and proudly cried, 'Look! Poopoo!' "

—BILL COSBY

BABIES "R" US

Popular Potty Seats

Baby Bjorn Toilet Trainer

First Stages 3-in-1 Potty

Fisher Price Royal Potty

Graco Training Rewards

Soft Seat Potty & Stepstool

Safety 1st Potty 'N Step Stool

Sesame Street Soft Potty Seat

TOT-CO Toilet Trainer

DID YOU KNOW?

The modern toilet was invented by Sir John Harington, who installed one for Queen Elizabeth I. Thomas Crapper later improved on the original design.

POTTY SEAT ADAPTERS

Most of the parents I coach prefer potty-chairs over seat adapters, but if you have a child who's fascinated by the adult toilet, a seat adapter can be the best way to go. (Literally!) Seat adapters are also great when you're traveling, shopping, or visiting friends. So, even if you initially teach your child to use a potty-chair, once she gets the hang of it you may want to introduce her to a seat adapter too.

There are various styles of seat adapters, but they all have the same purpose–to reduce the opening of the adult toilet seat to accomodate a child's bottom.

When you select a seat adapter for your child, keep in mind the same three secrets as for choosing a potty-chair– safety, size, and simplicity.

POTTY-CHAIR CLEAN-UP MADE SIMPLE!

1. Place a small amount of water or a few sheets of toilet paper at the bottom of the pot for easy clean-up of BMs.

2. Remember, never put bleach at the bottom of the pot. Urine contains ammonia, which, when combined with bleach, creates a chemical reaction producing toxic fumes. It is okay to use bleach to clean out the pot as a way of disinfecting.

3. Remove BMs immediately to prevent your child from playing with their feces.

4. Try to make your child a part of the clean-up process.

To make the best choice, consider the following questions:

Safety

1. Can this seat adapter be rocked or tipped off the adult toilet seat?
2. Can my child slide or fall off the side or back of this seat?
3. Are there any sharp, pointed, or protruding pieces that can scrape, scratch, puncture, or bruise my child?
4. Are there any parts that can move, slide, or pinch my child?

A lot of kids prefer the seat adapters that have handles because they feel more secure with something to hold on to. Handles can also make it easier to put on, take off, and carry.

Size

1. Will this seat adapter fit correctly and snugly on our toilet?
2. Is this seat adapter the correct size for my child's bottom?
3. Will this seat adapter fold up for easy transport?

Simplicity

1. Is this seat adapter lightweight and easy to put on and take off the toilet?
2. Does this seat adapter fold for easy carrying?
3. Is it easy to clean?

YOU CAN SAY THAT AGAIN!

"The best inheritance a person can give to his children is a few minutes of his time each day."

—O. A. BATTISTA

DID YOU KNOW?

A six-month supply of disposable pull-ups costs about $800 per child.

4. If the seat adapter has a safety shield, is it easy to remove and reattach?

FOOTSTOOLS

If your child is going to use a seat adapter, he also needs a footstool so he can step up to the adult toilet. But even if your child is learning with a potty-chair, footstools are great for helping kids reach the sink so they can wash their hands and brush their teeth. I suggest that parents buy a footstool for each bathroom that their child will be using.

Before you buy a footstool, make sure it

- Is wide enough not to wobble
- Has rubber floor grippers that securely grip and hold
- Is light enough for your child to easily lift and move

Lots of kids really like the footstools that double as storage containers because they can keep favorite toys and books in the bathroom.

Dolls

With the One-Day Potty-Training Party method, the doll is every bit as important as the potty-chair or seat adapter. The doll is essential because it plays a leading role in your child's learning process. Your child will learn how to use the potty *by teaching his doll.*

I've found it's helpful for boys to teach boy dolls and girls to teach girl dolls, mainly because they tend to identify more with a same-gender doll. Some parents choose to use dolls that are anatomically correct, but the majority of moms that attend my Potty-Training Boot Camps have successfully used dolls that are not.

Obviously, dolls that drink and wet can be good choices for the potty-training party, but some of these dolls can actually be more challenging to work with than nonwetting dolls. For example, some of them automatically wet when you sit them up. Others wet at random, and that doesn't work well for our purposes either. So, if you decide to go with a doll that wets, make sure you can control *when* it wets.

My favorite potty-training dolls are Emma and Paul, made by Corolle. They're vanilla scented, which kids love (so do the moms—and even the dads—in my Potty-Training Boot Camps), and they wet when you squeeze their bellies. An added bonus, if you're training a boy, is that Paul is anatomically correct.

You can also use a doll that doesn't wet. When I was showing my son how to teach Dolly to go pee-pee in the potty, I held a baby bottle filled with lemonade behind the doll's back and squirted it into the potty. Spencer got a big kick out of *hearing* Dolly go potty and seeing the yellow liquid in the potty-chair.

Although it's not essential, it can be fun to use a doll that fits the theme of the potty party you're planning. For instance, if you're having a TV character party because your son loves

---

EXPERTS SAY

One of the best ways to discourage potty mouth is to ignore it. Pretending not to hear your toddler say words like pooh-pooh butt and piss-head makes the "bad words" less exciting to the child. It reduces the chance that she'll test you with the four-letter variety.

SpongeBob, you can use a SpongeBob doll. If your daughter loves animals, you might have a zoo party and use a stuffed monkey. Monkeys work great because they're shaped like kids and can sit on the potty. I wouldn't recommend trying to potty train a stuffed elephant!

GRANDMA SAYS

It's not a bargain if it breaks.

Doll Clothes

- Fabric that goes with the party theme, cut into rectangular pieces to make twelve pairs of big-kid theme underpants; if you don't want to sew, you can secure the underpants with tape or theme-related Band-Aids
- Two skirts, dresses, pairs of shorts, or pants—the doll can just wear her big-kid theme underpants all day

Kid's Clothes

- One or two packages of training pants (with plastic exterior)
- One box of disposable "Pull Ons"
- One dozen pairs of big-kid underwear

GRANDMA SAYS

Never buy anything that has to be broken in to be comfortable.

For toddlers who demonstrate signs of potty-training readiness, the secret to rapid toilet-training progress is focusing on their excitement and pride of moving up from diapers to big-kid underwear.

POTTY PROGRESS CHARTS

- ◆ One for the doll
- ◆ One for your child

In any endeavor, it's easier to know how we're doing if we can measure and keep track of our progress. The same is true for learning to use the toilet, and that's why Potty Progress Charts are so important.

Decorate the progress charts with pictures that go with the party theme. Picture or drawings that remind your child of the celebration at the party's end work like a charm. For instance, if your celebration will be at Chuck E. Cheese's, put Chuck E. Cheese's picture on the charts.

Toddlers love "winning," even when there's no prize involved. But toss a few stars and stickers into the mix and you definitely up the ante! There's a thin line between bribing and rewarding, but the defining factor is whether or not your child is learning and having fun. In chapter five, I'll share some of the creative ideas—like the Mystery Present Box—that other moms have victoriously used on potty party day.

Most toddlers like all sorts of stickers, but to make earning the stickers more valuable, select stickers that you know your

EXPERTS SAY

Children whose parents praise their toilet-training progress and avoid using negative words and criticism graduate from diapers about three months sooner than their peers.

child will love. You can also choose stickers that go with your child's potty party theme. I'll give you some creative suggestions in chapter five.

FLUSHABLE WET WIPES

Most toddlers adore toilet paper! They love watching it roll off the dispenser onto the floor. They enjoy making long paper trails that originate in the bathroom and wind through the rest of the house. And they've been known to derive great pleasure in seeing how much toilet paper can be stuffed into the toilet.

However, very few toddlers are good at wiping themselves with toilet paper. So, to help your child do a better job of wiping and to avoid toilet paper waste, stock up on flushable wet wipes and keep the toilet paper where she can't reach it. (See "Toilet Paper Control Tips" in chapter four!)

PLASTIC MATTRESS COVERS

The secret to making nighttime accidents fast and easy to clean up is what I call double-making the bed. Double-making the bed means that you put two entire sets of sheets and plastic mattress covers on your child's bed.

When your child wets the bed in the middle of the night, all you have to do is pull off the top layer of sheets and mattress cover and voilà! The bed's made! Just put the blanket and bedspread back on and it's back to la-la land for you and your child.

EXPERTS SAY

Only 45 percent of girls and 35 percent of boys stay dry at night before age three.

How to Double-Make a Bed

1. Put on the plastic mattress cover
2. Put on the fitted sheet and top sheet
3. Put on another plastic mattress cover
4. Put on another fitted sheet and top sheet
5. Complete the bed with blankets and bedspread

4. potty party prerequisites
laying the foundation for success

What we learn with pleasure, we never forget.

—ALFRED MERCIER, novelist

Imagine what would happen if you tried to drive a car without knowing how to steer and without ever having seen anyone else drive? It might make an amusing movie, but in reality it would probably be a disaster! Before we can pass a driving test, we have to study the rules of the road and learn how to safely operate and maneuver a car. It's not a skill that just comes naturally, and it takes practice before we feel comfortable and confident.

The same idea holds true for a toddler who is learning to use the toilet. Because we are adults who have been successfully using the toilet for decades, it's easy to forget that there are certain things we need to teach our toddler *before* we begin the actual potty-training process. Remember that our definition for totally potty trained is when a child can get herself in and out of the bathroom, get her pants down and back up again, wipe herself adequately, and wash her hands—all with minimal assistance.

To lay the foundation for potty-training success, I highly recommend helping your child to master all of those individual skills before you teach him to use the potty itself. And that's where potty-party prerequisites come in. When your child begins to show some of the readiness signs described in chapter two, it's time to start working with the Potty-Training Building Blocks.

I should mention that even if your child is showing signs of readiness, he probably won't express an interest in using the potty until you provide him with that goal. While I don't recommend pushing a child to use the toilet, if your child is ready, begin talking to him about using the potty and let him know that you will be preparing him to graduate from diapers to big-boy pants.

Once your child shows signs of readiness, encourage her and give her direction. If she doesn't resist, she may be even more ready than you think. In fact, since toddlers love imitating big kids and adults, they may even approach toilet training with enthusiasm, particularly if you present the idea in a positive, exciting way.

Potty-Training Building Blocks

 ACTIONS SPEAK LOUDER THAN WORDS: MODELING

 BODY PARTS AND FUNCTIONS 101: WHAT WE CALL THEM AND HOW THEY WORK

CLEAN AND DRY: WIPING AND WASHING

 DRESSING AND UNDRESSING: ELASTIC BEATS THE PANTS OFF BUTTONS AND ZIPPERS

 EASY DOES IT! LEARNING TO LET YOUR CHILD LEARN

EXPERTS SAY

"Granted, I don't believe in *pushing* little ones into doing anything their bodies aren't ready for them to do, but at the same time, we need to present opportunities for children to learn. Sadly, parents are confused between two issues: behavior that needs to be taught and natural progression (developmental milestones that automatically happen)."

–TRACY HOGG, *SECRETS OF THE BABY WHISPERER FOR TODDLERS*

ACTIONS SPEAK LOUDER THAN WORDS

Studies have convincingly proven that children can be toilet trained significantly faster when their parents use a learning method called modeling. Basically, modeling means learning by watching and by teaching. This valuable research, conducted by Nathan H. Azrin, Ph.D., and Richard M. Foxx, Ph.D., showed that children who observed their parents, grandparents, older siblings, or other kids using the toilet were more interested and willing to try it themselves. The study also proved that children who *taught* a doll how to use the potty learned much faster themselves.

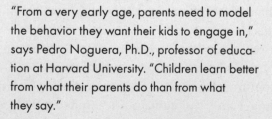

EXPERTS SAY

"From a very early age, parents need to model the behavior they want their kids to engage in," says Pedro Noguera, Ph.D., professor of education at Harvard University. "Children learn better from what their parents do than from what they say."

Do you remember the old adage about how you can lead a horse to water? It's even more apropos to our precious preschoolers and their potties. Trust me on this one. As you soon will discover (if you haven't already), buying and displaying a potty-chair or seat adapter does not mean your child will use it. In most cases, the direct link between the potty and elimination of waste must be taught and reinforced before children make the connection.

YOU CAN SAY THAT AGAIN!

"Children have never been very good at listening to their elders, but they have never failed to imitate them."

–JAMES BALDWIN, AUTHOR OF GO *TELL IT ON THE MOUNTAIN*

THREE TYPES OF MODELING

There are three types of modeling that can be used to help teach a child when and how to use the potty.

Role Modeling. Say Cheese! It will help your future *toileteer* a great deal if you allow him to watch as you, a sibling, preschool friend, or relative use the toilet. Demonstrating the elimination process is one of the most effective ways to teach your child about using the toilet. Regardless of whether your toddler is a girl or a boy, it will help for them to see men and women, boys and girls using the toilet. With that said, lots of kids are more interested in and motivated by someone of the same gender. My son Spencer was more motivated by urinating with his father, grandfathers, and little male cousins than with me or by himself.

Sometimes the desire to imitate older brothers and sisters or playgroup friends is stronger than the desire to imitate a parent. Oftentimes, an older sibling takes on a coaching role with the younger one, becoming a role model and a cheerleader rolled into one. The older sibling's victory chant is, "If I can do it, you can too!"

YOU CAN SAY THAT AGAIN!

"Role modeling is the most basic responsibility of parents. Parents are handing life's scripts to their children, scripts that in all likelihood will be acted out for the rest of the children's lives."

—STEPHEN R. COVEY, *THE 7 HABITS OF HIGHLY EFFECTIVE PEOPLE*

If the thought of your toddler observing you, up close and personal, use the toilet pushes your modesty or comfort zone too far, don't sweat it. A lot of men and women feel this way. You can find role models for your child who are closer to her age. You can also sit on the toilet seat fully clothed and explain what happens when grown-ups, big boys, and big girls use the toilet.

If you *do* feel comfortable let yourself be a little silly and have fun with this. The more relaxed and at home you are on the toilet, the more comfortable your child is likely to feel. You might show him how you keep some favorite magazines next to the toilet and ask him what books and toys he would put next to a potty of his own.

You can also let your toddler hear the sound of the urine or BM going into the toilet. Some parents really play this up. Remember the games you played when you were trying to feed him? "Here comes the airplane, *Zoooom!* Open wide."

YOU CAN SAY THAT AGAIN!

"Children have more need of models than of critics."

—CAROLYN COATS, *THINGS YOUR DAD ALWAYS TOLD YOU BUT YOU DIDN'T WANT TO HEAR*

Most kids get a kick out of hearing a BM splash in the toilet, so play it up. "Countdown to splash landing. Ready? 3, 2, 1, *splash*!"

When you have his complete attention (and you will), explain that this is where big people like Mommy, Daddy, Grandma, and Uncle Ed put their urine and BMs. Tell him, with enthusiasm—the same way you might tell him that he just won a pony—that *someday*, when he's ready to be a "big kid," you will buy him a special little potty all his own.

Spencer and I used to race each other to the bathroom (you'll learn this secret in chapter six), and one day as I dashed in and lifted the toilet seat for him, he said, "Momma, let's pee at the same time." He and his cousin had just spent the weekend together, and standing up to pee together had become a fun sort of game. I said, "Well, honey, I'm a girl and you know I sit down when I have to go pee-pee because I have a vagina. You and your cousins are all boys, so you can all stand up because you all have a penis. And Daddy can stand up, too, because he has a penis just like you." Spencer looked at me for a second and I could see the wheels turning to formulate a question or observation. (All moms know this look!) He looked down at his penis, started giggling, and said, "Papa doesn't have a penis just like me. He has a big giant papa-size pee-pee."

Now is also the time to begin introducing and modeling rules of good etiquette. Teach your toddler to clean up any splashes of urine that didn't make it into the potty and put down the toilet seat. Show her how you wipe the water splashes off the sink so it's dry and shiny for the next person to use. Initially, try to keep the rules to a minimum and make sure they're basic enough for your toddler to follow.

Book and Video Modeling. Books and videos are great teaching tools and a fun way to begin conversations with your child about her body, body functions, and using the toilet. The great thing about books and videos is that they illustrate the training process from beginning to end. Plus, each time you

CELEBRITY SCOOP

The five-year-old niece of actress Betty Grable once asked her aunt if she could join her in the bathtub. When Grable agreed, the child climbed into the tub. Grable noticed that her niece was staring at her body and asked if anything was wrong. "No," the child answered. "I was just wondering why I'm so plain and you're so fancy."

read the book with your child or watch the video, the positive message of using the toilet is strengthened and reinforced.

I've listed a few of my favorites below. Look in the Resources section at the back of the book for a complete list of recommended books and videos.

Everyone Poops. Taro Gomi and Amanda Mayer Stinchecum (Kane/Miller Publishing, 1993). This book illustrates how literally *everything poops* in terms a little one can understand. My son loves this book and never tires of reading it—even to this day. We pretend the poop smells and say things like, "Oh, phewee." We both pinch our noses closed and he always cracks up laughing and says, "Read it again, Mom." If a child is laughing, he is learning.

When You've Got to Go! (Bear in the Big Blue House). Mitchell Kriegman and Kathryn Mitter, illustrator (Simon Spotlight, 2000). If your toddler's hero is Bear, you will both enjoy this story.

Once Upon a Potty. Alona Frankel (HarperCollins Juvenile Books, 1999). This adorable classic is available in boy and girl formats. It introduces babies and toddlers to a new potty.

My Big Boy Potty and My Big Girl Potty. Joanna Cole and Maxie Chambliss (HarperCollins Juvenile Books, 2000). Joanna Cole is a very talented writer of books for both children and adults. These books in particular are worthy of previewing. The theme is practice makes perfect, and it leaves your child with the feeling that he or she can do this too.

The Gas We Pass: The Story of Farts (My Body Science). Shinta Cho and Amanda Mayer Stinchecum (Kane/Miller Book Publishers, 1994). Just about every kid I know loves this book. And parents love it too because it teaches solid facts and gives kids great information. The authors tell it like it is and their blunt approach makes both toddlers and adults laugh.

Bear in the Big Blue House–Potty Time with Bear. Mitchell Kriegman, director (Columbia Tristar Home Video, 1999). A great supplement to the book. This is a no-pressure, when-you-are-ready and everybody-does-it approach. My son and I would dance and sing around the room when we played this video. It also has great tunes like "Welcome and Goodbye" and "Potty Chair."

I Gotta Go! (Vickilew, 2004). This award-winning program playfully and effectively supports the potty-training process from beginning to end. The video has a bonus CD that allows you to take the fun and inspiration on the road. I especially like the products of Vickilew because this company is committed to the development of positive, nonviolent, and empowering entertainment for children and families. Check out their website at www.vickilew.com or call 1-888-842-5458. Have your library order a copy if they don't own one already.

Doll Modeling. Using a doll that pees helps your child make the connection that the liquids we drink go down into our bellies and then come out again—into the potty if we're a big boy or big girl.

The doll will serve three very important purposes on potty party day. First, your child will relax and have fun teaching the doll to use the potty, and as she does so, she will learn herself. Second, it won't hurt your child's self-esteem when you reprimand the doll for going poopy in his big boy pants. (In chapter six, I give you step-by-step instructions for how to use the doll.) And third, your child's confidence in her ability to use the potty will grow as she helps and watches the doll doing it. "If my doll can learn to go potty, I can too."

YOU CAN SAY THAT AGAIN!

"If you would thoroughly know anything, teach it to others."

—TRYON EDWARDS, AMERICAN THEOLOGIAN

BODY PARTS AND FUNCTIONS 101

Along with teaching your toddler to recognize the sensations that mean "I have to use the potty," you need to teach him the words to use for his body parts and functions. Parents have invented dozens of words for body parts and the elimination process. Most experts recommend teaching children the correct names, but some parents just can't warm up to this approach. From what I've seen, the most important point to be made about word choice is consistency. You and your husband should decide on and use one word for urine, bowel movement, penis, vagina, and anus.

It will confuse your child if you ask her if she has to go tinkle in the morning and then call it pee-pee in the afternoon. In your search for an inoffensive term, please remember that children have very concrete thinking. A euphemism like "Do you have to go to the bathroom?" will probably be literally translated to "Do you need to *walk into* the bathroom?" Which means—unless there's something in the bathroom that your child needs—she will probably say no. Kids at this age rarely understand that "Do you need to go to the bathroom?" really means "Do you feel the urge to urinate or have a bowel movement?" The chart on page 56 may help you choose terms you can use together.

Whether you use the politically correct terminology or not, as long as your child knows what you mean, you'll both be okay. When I mention the word "penis" or "vagina" in my Potty-

★ TERMS CHART ★	
TEXTBOOK TERMS	POPULAR WORDS
Buttocks and Anus	Bottom, Bummy, Duppa, Tush
Penis	Pee-Pee, Peeper, Privates, Thing
Vagina	Bagina, Bottom, Gina, Privates, Yoni
Toilet	Potty, Pot
Urine	Pee, Pee-Pee, Tinkle, Wee-Wee, Wiz
Feces and Stool	Ka-Ka, Poop, Poo-Poo, Poopy, Do-Do, DooPah

Training Boot Camps, some of the adults in the class suddenly start acting like they're on an elevator. They look up at the ceiling, down at their feet, clear their throats, and look genuinely uncomfortable.

Much of this anxiety stems from a sense of shame that was instilled in a lot of us at a young age by our parents, teachers, or the neighborhood kids. When I was growing up, I never felt comfortable using the textbook terms for privates. I would rather have cut off my arm than utter the P or V word. And even as adults, some of us recoil at the thought of revealing the baby name our mom or dad used for our vagina or penis.

Thank goodness times are changing! Our generation takes a much more matter-of-fact approach that's helping kids grow up with fewer inhibitions.

When you come up with these words, you may just decide it's easier or makes sense to go with the experts' guidance. I mean, think about it; you never even considered telling your baby that his hands were called "wavies" or "clap claps." When she pointed to her nose and asked for a name, you didn't blush

FROM THE MOUTHS OF BABES

"When my two-and-a-half-year old son was watching my sister change her daughter's diaper, he exclaimed, 'Look Mommy, Alexis has two butts!' "

—NANCY MYERS

and say, "Ah . . . honey, that's your sniffer or sneezer." The truth is that there isn't a word in existence that will embarrass a three-year-old, unless he's learned by your explanation or re-action that it's a bad or offensive word. The more comfortable you are with the words you're using, the more natural your child will feel about using those words too.

If you really can't get yourself to use the real word, it's okay. Don't let the words become a big issue. Just be consistent with the terms that you decide to use. And, if your child is in daycare or spending time with other tots, don't be surprised if she adds a new word to her vocabulary that you haven't been using at home.

POTTY-TRAINING BOOT CAMP TIP

It's a good idea to choose words that are appropriate in your home and also with neighborhood playmates, child care providers, and grandparents. If all the other kids call it "going potty," your child may feel embarrassed calling it something else.

CLEAN AND DRY: WIPING AND WASHING

Silly as it may sound, "hygiene habits last a lifetime" illustrates another potty-party prerequisite. The first hygiene building block is teaching a boy to wipe his anus and dry his penis, and teaching a girl to wipe her vagina and her anus. The second is teaching your child to wash his hands. Once your child actually starts using a potty-chair, you'll also want to teach her to rinse the potty bowl and flush the toilet after each use. The more you allow your child to practice these new skills, the sooner she will adopt them as habits and be able to do them on her own.

DID YOU KNOW?

It takes fifteen to twenty-five seconds of washing with warm soapy water to dislodge microscopic bacteria and viruses.

WASHING HANDS

You can begin teaching your child how to wash his hands months before you host his potty party day. Let him stand on a footstool at the sink and watch while you wash *your* hands. Then take his hands in yours and gently wash them. Next encourage him to wash them himself, guiding him to wash each finger and thumb, the tops of his hands and the palms, and the spaces in between his fingers. Next teach him how to rinse all the soap off his hands, and use the towel to dry them.

GRANDMA SAYS

Buy a few fingernail brushes that are shaped like animals, encourage your child to name them, and teach her how to use them.

Hygiene Hints:

- Insist that hands be washed with soap and warm water after each bathroom use. Do not leave your child alone

with instructions to "wash your hands" until you know
he can do a very efficient job.

- Lots of kids rush the hand washing, so to teach them how
  long it takes to do it right; encourage them to sing the
  first verse of "Twinkle, Twinkle, Little Star" or "Happy
  Birthday" while washing.
- Demonstrate each step and practice together.
  - Use sturdy footstool to reach sink
  - Turn on water faucet
  - Wet hands
  - Soap hands
  - Rinse hands
  - Dry thoroughly with hand towel

To make sure that your child isn't burned by hot water, set
your water heater to a maximum of 120° Fahrenheit. To test the
temperature, turn on the hot water only and hold your hand
under the faucet. If you can't comfortably hold your hand under
the faucet, the water is too hot.

Use fun liquid soap pump containers that have characters on
the bottle or little floaties inside. A liquid dispenser is easier for
a child to handle, and they also help avoid slippery soap es-
capades. You can pick up a variety of styles at stores such as
Bed, Bath and Beyond. This makes washing fun and keeps a
child from getting bored with the learning process. You might
buy a variety of dispensers and rotate them so that there's a different one every day or so.

To keep your hand towels off the floor, attach a hand towel to
the towel bar with a shower curtain clip. This puts the towel
within your child's view and reach and eliminates a typical
bathroom tug-of-war.

WIPING

You can begin teaching your child to wipe by involving her in the process when you change her diaper. In the beginning, do the first big wipe yourself, and then invite your child to pull a hand wipe from the container and show her how to wipe her vagina and anus by gently holding her hand and guiding it through the motions. With practice and patience, your child will eventually get the hang of how to hold the wipe and how to clean an area that he can't see. If you're finding it frustrating or hard to believe that your child is struggling to learn wiping, I have a challenge for you. For one entire day, wipe yourself only with the opposite hand. I think you'll soon remember that it's only easy once you know how to do it.

◆ Explain that to make sure she is clean, she should keep using fresh pieces of toilet paper until there are no more brown marks.

◆ Teach children—especially girls—to wipe from front to back to prevent infections.

◆ Allow your child to use flushable baby wipes after bowel movements. It cuts down on laundry and helps them to do a better job too.

Even after your child learns to wipe himself, you will need to stay involved until he truly masters the skill. Meanwhile, be careful not to wrinkle up your nose or make comments like "icky" or "stinky" when changing a diaper or helping them to wipe themselves. If a child learns to feel uncomfortable with her body or thinks anything related to her privates is shameful, those ideas can have a negative effect on her self-esteem and even on her adult relationships.

This is also a good time to start teaching your child that big kid poop and grown-up poop goes in the toilet. You can help your child to make the connection between his BMs and the toilet by taking the full diaper into the bathroom, dumping the contents into the toilet, and explaining, "This is where big-kid BMs go." If your child isn't afraid to flush the toilet, invite him to do the honor.

DID YOU KNOW?

The American Society of Microbiologists conducted a study in 2005 by observing what people did (or didn't do) in public restrooms. They found that on average, only 82 percent of those using the toilet washed their hands afterward. Yikes! With all those people skipping basic hygiene, you might want to show your kids how to open a public restroom door with a paper towel or piece of toilet paper!

Playing with Poop

I know what you're thinking. I hear it all the time in my potty boot camps—seeing a child playing with his feces is disgusting! First of all, try to remember that unless you change your toddler's diaper the instant after she has a bowel movement, she's accustomed to the smell of her own poop, and it probably doesn't smell offensive to her. Sort of like how we can handle it when *we* pass gas, but if someone else does it we gag!

Second, there's some truth to the adage "One man's junk is another man's treasure." Think about it. To a child, poop is a free and unlimited source of entertainment. Just like Play-Doh, it works well for rolling, molding, and pounding. It's tacky and squishy and, to them, fun to squeeze between their fingers. The opportunities are endless.

Most experts agree that a simple "No, we do not play with that" will suffice. Then immediately take your child to the bathroom and very carefully wash his hands with soap and warm water. Do not forget to clean under the fingernails. Fascination with feces is not a rare occurrence among toddlers, so thank the potty gods that this stage—like gas—eventually passes!

GRANDMA SAYS

If you want your child to learn that what goes in his mouth comes out his bottom, just show him his BM the day after he eats corn.

Try to remember that this is a learning stage and it's best not to refer to her "poop art" as gross or dirty. If you do, she may feel these words apply to her or her creativity instead of describing the raw material she's using.

Without shaming her, explain that the poop we make comes from the food we eat. Whatever our body doesn't need to be strong and healthy comes out of our bottom and goes into the potty.

POTTY-TRAINING BOOT CAMP TIP

 If your child is a poop artist, supply her with other squishy materials to play with, like Play-Doh, nontoxic clay, finger paints, and Edible Mud.

EDIBLE MUD RECIPE

2 egg yolks
3 cups milk
3 tablespoons flour
1 cup sugar
5 tablespoons cocoa

Beat egg yolks in a medium-size saucepan. Add milk and stir well. In a bowl, mix flour, sugar, and cocoa together. Add this mixture to the milk and yolks in the saucepan. Cook over medium-high heat until it begins bubbling.

Turn heat to medium-low and cook two to three more minutes to make sure the eggs are thoroughly cooked. Remove from heat and pour into small bowls or ice cube trays until cool. (Edible Mud can be covered and stored in the refrigerator for three days.)

DRESSING AND UNDRESSING: ELASTIC BEATS THE PANTS OFF BUTTONS AND ZIPPERS

Clothing that is easy to pull up and down is the key to enhancing your child's ability to get his pants down in time to use the potty and back up again afterward.

POTTY-TRAINING BOOT CAMP TIP

 An ingenious mother who couldn't bear not dressing her son in his adorable suspender outfit removed the strap clips and sewed on Velcro tabs.

---

* Select loose-fitting clothes, such as oversize jeans or warm-up pants for boys and rompers or skirts for girls.
* Choose elastic waistbands.
* Avoid zippers, snaps, belts, buttons, buckles, and suspenders.

GRANDMA SAYS

 When a shirt hangs down too low and hinders a child from pulling down his pants, gather the shirt at the back and secure it with a large safety pin or rubber band.

EASING THE FEAR OF FLUSHING

If your child is frightened by a flushing toilet—many children are—it's important to acknowledge and address his fears. The sound and force of the swirling water can be very scary and upsetting to children, and many worry about being "swallowed alive." Parents should never tease or ridicule a child for being afraid of a new unknown.

Determine what your child is frightened or upset by. Is it

a. The sound of gushing water?

b. The way the water looks when it's swirling in the tank?

c. Falling into the toilet, and/or being sucked down with the flush?

d. The fear of something coming up through the toilet and biting or grabbing the child?

e. Losing a part of himself by flushing a bowel movement?

One of the secrets to avoiding and alleviating all of the above fears is to teach your child about the toilet. Just like adults, kids sometimes fear what they don't understand. So, it's time for Toilet Class!

TOILETS 101: AN INTRODUCTORY COURSE FOR TODDLERS

Begin by turning off the water valves at the base of the toilet. Remove the lid from the toilet tank. Show your child the water in the back of the tank. Explain that when the toilet is flushed, the dirty water in the toilet bowl goes down the drain—just like the water in the bathtub goes down the drain. Tell him that the clean water in the tank goes into the toilet bowl. Invite him to push the flush handle. Many children who are upset by the sound of the flushing toilet or the way the water looks when it swirls around in the toilet bowl feel more at ease if they get to control the flushing. If he doesn't want to, assure him that it's okay not to want to push the flush handle and tell him you're going to do it.

So that the flush doesn't surprise or catch him off guard, and to create some positive excitement, say something like, "I am the Master Flusher and on the count of three, I'm going to flush this toilet. [Invite him to count with you.] One . . . two . . . three . . . flush!" Then clap your hands, shout "Yay!" and encourage your child to join in on the celebration.

Take a minute to ask him if he has questions about what just happened. Then, invite him to flush the toilet. "Do you want to be the Master Flusher and get to be the one who flushes the toilet this time?" If he says yes, start with the count: One, two, three, flush! and praise him profusely when he flushes the toilet. Give each other high-fives and tell him he did a great job. If he says no, repeat the process yourself.

Since you turned off the water valves at the beginning of class, when the toilet is flushed again there won't be any water in the tank to fill the toilet bowl. This will allow you to give your child an up close and personal look at the hole in the bottom of the toilet. One of the reasons "the hole" is so scary to kids is that it's hidden at the back of the toilet bowl and they can't see what it really looks like or how big it is.

Take a plastic ball that's a little larger than the hole in the bottom of your toilet (find a ball the right size ahead of time). Show your child that the ball is *bigger* than the hole. Show him that the ball is *smaller* than his bottom and his head. Explain that if the ball can't fit through the hole in the toilet, neither can he. (The book *When You've Got to Go!* [Bear in the Big Blue House] does a great job of introducing children to the way toilets work. So, if playing "plumber" for a day doesn't appeal to you or you fear getting in over your head, sit with your child and read the book together, and then take him into the bathroom and review what you both read in the book.)

Some kids are really afraid that a wild animal, spider, snake, or something equally disagreeable is going to come up through the toilet and grab or bite them. So, the next point to cover in Toilets 101 is that things can *only* go *down* the toilet and that nothing can *ever* come *up*. Turn the water valves at the base of the toilet back on and let the toilet tank fill up with water. Once again, offer to let him flush the toilet, and repeat the counting sequence. As the toilet is flushing, show him that when the water comes into the toilet, it comes in at the top of the bowl. Explain that the only thing in the water tank is water and that water is the only thing that can fit in through the tiny holes at the top of the toilet bowl.

The final point to cover is more about psychology than plumbing. It's not uncommon for a toddler to think of her bowel movements as part of her body. The sound of a bowel movement "falling out" of her bottom can be scary, and the idea of flushing it away can be traumatic. Help your child to understand that we call bowel movements "waste" because they are something our bodies make that we are supposed to "throw away." Explain that it started out as food and now that her body has used up all the good stuff in the food, it's time to get rid of the rest.

For lots of kids, all it takes is a calm explanation and the acknowledgment that they are experiencing a sense of loss. Sometimes just waving bye bye to the bowel movement before flushing it is enough to make them feel okay about it. If your child continues to feel upset by this part of the process, don't worry. Just wait until he leaves the bathroom and flush the toilet for him. Eventually, he'll flush it on his own.

- Girls can go panty-free under a dress or skirt and boys might try shorts without underwear.
- Girls and boys can go bare-bottomed all day during summer months and inside during the winter, if you turn up the heat.

On the day of the potty party and for a few weeks afterward, consider letting your child wear undershirts (rather than T-shirts), at least around the house. Many children's shirts are just long enough to get in between your child's privates and the potty! Undershirts tend to be shorter and stay out of the way.

A great video that helps your toddler learn how to dress herself is *All By Myself, Getting Dressed* by Lady Bug Productions. Find out more at www.allbymyself.com.

EASY DOES IT! LEARNING TO LET YOUR CHILD LEARN

For the past two and a half to three years or more, you have been a primary caregiver for your child. That means you're used to doing things for her and you've probably learned how to do them quickly, neatly, and efficiently. Congratulations! Seriously. But now, it's time to reverse gears for a while and slow the whole show down. After mastering the art of speed, your brain may have a hard time agreeing that, at least for a while, slower is better. It really helps if you don't think of this as losing ground or going backward, especially if you're a type-A, action-driven mom!

If you want to create an atmosphere that is highly conducive to learning for your child, you have to begin to do less and allow him to do more—even though it takes longer and is a little messier.

EXPERTS SAY

Low-achieving kids learn new behaviors better and faster when their parents offer them the appropriate amount of guidance and encourage them in a positive way. Researchers at the University of Illinois studied 110 moms and their children. The researchers concluded that what low-achievers need most is for parents to help them build confidence in their abilities.

Preparing *Yourself* for Your Child's Learning Curve

PATIENCE IS A VIRTUE

Actually, at this stage of your child's development, patience is much more than a virtue. It's an essential sanity survival tool! Constantly remind yourself that there's no way your child can complete tasks as quickly as you can. Resist the urge to rush him or jump in and do things for him. Be aware of your body language and vocal expressions too. If your child is putting everything she has into wiping up the bathroom counter—even if it takes ten minutes—don't start sighing or huffing and puffing, and don't stand over her with your hands on your hips or other body postures that show you're tired of waiting or upset. Instead, praise her progress, leave the bathroom, and then check back every couple of minutes to see how she's doing.

YOU CAN SAY THAT AGAIN!

"The key to everything is patience. You get the chicken by hatching the egg, not by smashing it."

—ARNOLD H. GLASGOW, AMERICAN AUTHOR

BUILD TIME CUSHIONS INTO EVERY TASK

If you really want your child to learn new skills and habits, you have to give him time to do so and you can't do that if you're always in a hurry. If it takes you five minutes to dress your toddler and now he's learning to dress himself, plan for at least ten or fifteen minutes.

DIVIDE AND CONQUER

When you really *do* have to pick up the pace, divide the tasks between you and your child. "You flush the toilet and I'll wipe off the counter around the sink." Or, "You wash your hands and I'll empty and clean the potty bowl."

FOCUS ON WHAT YOUR CHILD IS DOING RIGHT!

In the process of teaching our children something new, we sometimes spend so much time trying to correct what's "wrong," that we forget to acknowledge the things they're doing right. Every day, catch your child doing something well, and show her your pride and pleasure by giving her sincere praise.

EMPOWER YOUR CHILD'S DECISION-MAKING PROCESS

Practice giving your child choices so he can practice making decisions. Begin by giving your child options that are win-win situations. For instance, you might ask, "Would you like to wear your green shirt or your blue shirt?" knowing that either one is fine. You can also use this strategy with tasks. "Would you rather put your toys in the toy chest or put your dirty clothes in the hamper?"

PRACTICE MAKES PERFECT

If your child can put on her own shoes, let her do it most of the time. (Just think of it as another chance for you to perfect the virtue of patience!) The more often you let her do things herself, the better she will become at doing them (and the faster) and the less you will have to do for her. In Zen-Speak, it's the difference between giving your child a fish and teaching her to fish.

DON'T PROJECT YOUR FEELINGS ON YOUR CHILD

If standing by and waiting for your child to successfully pull up his big-boy underpants and corduroys feels like Chinese water torture to you, keep in mind that his perspective may be quite different from yours. So don't jump in and thrust your help upon him unless he asks for it, or he's showing visible signs of frustration.

PRAISE "GOOD ENOUGH" EFFORTS AS *GREAT*!

If your toddler manages to get both shoes on the right feet but happens to put on two different color socks, so what? Keep your attention and focus on what's most important—which, in this case, is the fact that your child, who used to be totally dependent on you for dressing him, is now learning to dress himself. The word of the day—matching socks or not—is *bravo*! There really are very few things more destructive and debilitating to children as parents who continually express their angst and disappointment about a child's behavior or progress.

DON'T TAKE IT PERSONALLY

When a toddler disregards an order issued by Mom, Dad, a day-care provider, or any other authority figure, it's not a personal affront to that individual. Children learn by testing their boundaries and limits. Remember that you are the adult and you have to be the one to demonstrate maturity. So don't get pulled into power struggles with your toddler. Explain and educate, but don't negotiate! If we say, "It's time to sit on the potty," our child's most natural response just might be no. If we end the sentence by asking, "understood?" our child answers *that* question, typically with the word "yes."

In her syndicated column, Dr. Sylvia Rimm advises, "For is-

CELEBRITY SCOOP

Actress Jane Kaczmarek, the mom on *Malcolm in the Middle*, says that instead of saying it's time for bed, she says, "We're going to bed now. Understood?" Great advice!

sues like having her help you pick up toys or getting ready for bed, say things like, 'Right after we pick up your toys, we can have a story,' or 'After you're in your jammies, we'll have a snack.' The story and snack aren't exactly rewards, but help children understand the progression of activities so they're motivated to do them. You'll notice that preschool teachers use this approach."

Always keep uppermost in your mind that your child truly wants to please you and desperately needs your acceptance, praise, and love. Even when children at this age appear to be bucking the system or acting rebelliously, they are not trying to make your life more difficult. In most cases, they are simply learning by making mistakes, which is the most normal and natural way for children to learn.

5. hip hip hooray! it's potty party day!

Nothing great was ever achieved without enthusiasm.

—RALPH WALDO EMERSON

For months (or at least weeks), you've been planning and preparing for your child's potty-training party. So, I suggest that you start the day by congratulating yourself for everything that you've already accomplished. Then, take a few moments—before you even get out of bed—to picture how pleased and proud you and your child will both be when he uses the potty. Consider the fact that this day, filled with fun, excitement, and accomplishment, will be an incredible bonding experience for you and your child. It will also be one of the most significant days in your toddler's early childhood development.

First and foremost, potty training is a *learning* process, not a *disciplinary* process. Simply put, your child needs to understand what you want her to do before she can learn how to do it. The potty-training party is designed to be a fun, effective, and practical program that respects a child's capacity for self-learning and shares the responsibility of teaching and learning with the child.

No matter which party theme you've chosen, all potty parties use the same variety of teaching methods, modeling, and hands-on experience. This chapter provides a generic framework into which you can plug the particulars of your chosen theme party.

CELEBRITY SCOOP

"Potty training was a little hard. My daughter was the difficult one. Had no problem with me cleaning her tail just forever."

—JADA PINKETT SMITH, ACTRESS

The idea of potty training a toddler in one day gained popularity in the early 1970s when two psychologists, Nathan H. Azrin, Ph.D., and Richard M. Foxx, Ph.D., did some groundbreaking research on toilet-training procedures and the learning process. Azrin and Foxx developed educational programs that they called learning by imitation and learning by teaching. Their book, *Toilet Training in Less Than a Day*, was based on their research findings.

Some people criticized the method prescribed in the book and others found it fast and easy. This can probably be said about every potty-training book, including this one. Consequently, one of your most important roles as a parent is making sure that your child has the physical, cognitive, emotional, and social skills needed to succeed before you try any potty-training approach.

One of the reasons that potty-training parties are so successful is that we use a variety of approaches to help children learn.

YOU CAN SAY THAT AGAIN!

"To teach is to learn twice."

—JOSEPH JOUBERT (1754–1824),
FRENCH PHILOSOPHER AND AUTHOR

They learn by observing, listening, and doing. Their eyes, ears, and hands all participate in the educational process.

Sometimes parents are concerned that their child won't buy into the imagination aspect of the theme parties or the idea that their new doll is going pee-pee or poopy. If you share this concern, relax. Toddlers have very expansive imaginations and they adore playing make-believe. Kids at this age have what might be described as creativity running wild. These are the same kids who put cookies and milk out for Santa, believe that a giant rabbit brings them candy on Easter, and think of Sponge-Bob SquarePants as a peer. They delight in dressing up and wearing costumes, and they love to pretend they're doing whatever they see older kids and adults doing. Thus, the popularity of toy power tools, vacuum cleaners, washing machines, lawn mowers, vanity sets, musical instruments, golf clubs, and ovens.

Your toddler's imagination will easily accept that a banana is a microphone, a blanket is a magic carpet, and that her doll can pee and poop. The challenge isn't getting your child to believe in the make-believe scenarios, it's allowing yourself to really get into playing and pretending.

Essentially, your child will learn to use the potty by teaching his new doll to use the potty. Your role is to lead and guide the process, stick with the program, and enthusiastically reward the doll and your child for every step of progress.

POTTY-TRAINING BOOT CAMP TIP

It's a truism of hardened potty-training veterans that adults don't really teach children to go potty. Children teach themselves by teaching their dolls.

Potty Party Checklist

- Acquire all items on the Potty-Training Essentials List (chapter three).
- Purchase the items on your chosen party theme list (chapter five).
- Buy and wrap a present for yourself that you really want.
- Wrap the doll.
- Wrap and hide your child's big-kid underwear.
- Cut fabric or alter big-kid underwear to make a dozen big-kid underpants for the doll—these underpants should match or have the same theme as your child's big-kid underwear.
- Place the potty-chair in the bathroom.
- Decorate the bathroom and party room with the chosen theme.
- Wrap party prizes.
- Wrap your child's Grand Finale Big Kid Celebration gifts from you and your family members.
- Prepare a variety of enticing bite-size treats.
- Stash a handful of potty-training books in the bathroom and a handful in the party room.
- Stack the potty-training videos next to the VCR.
- Purchase a variety of drinks and prepare the ingredients to make fruit smoothies (see recipes later in this chapter).
- Place the waterproof blanket or rug on the sofa in the party room.

In the next chapter, I'll provide you with all the details that you need to prepare for the big day, and I'll give you twelve party themes to choose from. Before beginning the party, review the Potty Party Checklist to be sure you're ready and have everything you need. By taking care of all party decorations, treats, prizes, and drinks ahead of time, you can give your full attention to your child and stay focused on helping him learn daytime bladder and bowel control by the end of the day.

In addition to preparing for the party, make arrangements so that you and the child you're potty training will be the only two people at home while the learning stages of the potty party are in progress (from morning until around 6 P.M.). If you have other children, plan for your husband, a relative, or a baby-sitter to take care of them somewhere other than at your house until it's time for the Grand Finale Big Kid Celebration.

Potty Party Secrets

- Keep the potty party a secret until your child wakes up on the day of the party.

- The more enthusiastic and excited you are, the more positively your child will respond to potty training his doll and using the potty himself.

- Do not ask your child any yes or no questions. You never want to give her a chance to say no. Instead, use the suggestion/command technique discussed later in the chapter.

- Prepare bite-size food treats and irresistible drinks. You'll find lots of ideas perfect for every theme in the next chapter.

- Empower your child with plenty of positive reinforcement.

- Remember that the morning of the potty party is all about potty training the doll. Don't ask your child to sit on the potty and don't correct him or show disapproval when he urinates or has a bowel movement in his diaper. His big-boy transformation doesn't occur until after lunch.

♦ To teach your child that big kids don't urinate or have bowel movements in their underpants, reprimand and correct the doll. Never criticize or reprimand your child.

EXPERTS SAY

Spanking a child may lead to more trouble down the road. Researchers from Johns Hopkins Bloomberg School of Public Health in Baltimore, Maryland, followed 1,966 children from birth until they entered elementary school. They discovered that the kids ages two and younger who were physically disciplined at least once a week (39 percent) were about twice as likely to have behavior problems four years later that required the parents to meet with a teacher. Kids who were spanked five times a week were four times more likely to have behavior issues.

Rise and Shine: Potty Party Morning

During the first half of the potty party, your child will teach the doll to use the potty-chair. You will lead and guide your child to teach the doll.

When your toddler wakes up, greet him with an enthusiastic "Good morning!" Tell him that you saw a surprise for him in the bathroom. Race him to the bathroom and let him discover the wrapped package containing the new doll wearing themed underwear.

As soon as your child opens the package, get really excited about the doll. Act like you are surprised by it too and immediately lead the child to name the doll. "Wow, Jonathan. What a cool present! You got a doll. What should we name it?"

Once your child has named the doll, suggest that you all go into the kitchen for breakfast. Interact with the doll. Talk *to* it directly and talk *about* it with your child.

When your child finishes breakfast, direct him to the designated party room by saying, "Come on, Bobby, let's go read Dolly a book!" Rush off with your child and the doll to the party room and quickly choose one of the potty-training books to read to Dolly. You'll find specific suggestions based on the twelve themes in the next chapter. Hop up on the couch that you've covered with the waterproof blanket or rug and have your child hop up and sit next to you. Place the doll between you and your child.

The secret is to give your child and the doll your total attention all morning as you keep the pace of the party moving from one activity to the next. In between reading books, watching potty-training videos, and playing games, you are leading your child to take his doll to the potty, check its big-kid underpants to see if they are wet or dry, and correct the doll when it goes pee-pee or poop in its big-kid underpants. Your child discovers, through your enthusiasm, that being a big kid and wearing big-kid underwear is a really big deal! Your child participates in praising the doll and giving it treats, stickers, and prizes when she goes on the potty and when she keeps her underpants dry and poop free.

Read a book or play a game, then say something like, "Come on, Kathy, I think Dolly has to go pee-pee in the potty." Grab the doll and race your child into the bathroom. Guide your child to help pull down

---

WORKING WITH THE DOLL

If you have a doll that wets on command, make sure its bladder (water reservoir) is full enough to allow it to urinate when you put it on the potty. Find out ahead of time how much the doll has to drink to make it urinate and make sure you give it enough liquid so that it's ready to go when you choose.

If you're using a doll that doesn't wet or you're using a stuffed animal, you can make it urinate in the potty by using this lemonade trick: fill a small baby bottle or squirt bottle with lemonade and hide it behind the potty chair. When your child puts the doll on the potty, distract him by asking him to get the wet wipes or toilet paper on the other side of the bathroom. As soon as he turns his back, while hiding the bottle behind the doll's back, squirt the lemonade into the potty and exclaim, "Georgie, Dolly just went pee-pee in the potty." (It's very important that your child doesn't see you squirt the liquid into the potty, so if you use a dolly or stuffed toy that doesn't wet on its own, you'll need to be very smooth about keeping this trick a secret!)

the doll's pants and put her on the potty. Then make the doll wet. As soon as the doll pees, make a huge fuss over it.

Get really excited and proclaim, "Look, Kathy, Dolly went pee-pee on the potty!" Clap your hands and dance around as if you just won the million-dollar lottery. Show your child the doll's Potty Progress Chart that you've put up in the bathroom and let her choose a sticker to put on Dolly's chart to show that she went pee-pee on the potty. (Don't even think that you can get away with using the old stickers that your child has already seen and played with before. Get a variety of stickers that you know your child will love.)

After your child puts the sticker on Dolly's chart, cheer for Dolly and say, "Dolly's a big girl! Let's go get Dolly a treat!" Then, grab Dolly with one hand and your child's hand with the other and rush to the treat tray you have prepared and hidden.

Select a treat for the doll or let your child pick one out. (Remember that the treats are bite-size morsels!) Don't calmly suggest that your child pick out a treat for the doll. You want to gush with enthusiasm as you say, "Brian, let's give Dolly a treat since she went pee-pee on the potty! Pick out a treat for Dolly!" When your child selects the treat, hold it up to the doll's mouth and repeat why the doll is getting the treat. "Dolly is such a big boy. He went pee-pee on the potty and now he gets a treat."

Obviously, the doll can't really eat the treat, so as you're holding it up to the doll's mouth, say to your child, "You know what? You can have Dolly's treat if *someday* you'll go pee-pee on the potty like Dolly did. Will you promise to go pee-pee on the potty *someday* just like Dolly?" "Someday" is the operative word here. And although your child doesn't know it, someday is just a few hours from now!

If your child already uses the potty sometimes, replace "someday" with the words "every time."

Your child will want the treat, so he'll be happy to agree to the "someday" scenario. This makes a positive link in his mind between using the potty and feeling good and happy.

After your child eats the treat, shout, "Yay! Dolly's such a big girl! Let's go read her another book!" Then pick up the doll and skip, hop, or race back to the party room.

STAYING DRY

Read the doll a book, play a game, or watch a potty-training video, then direct your child to check the doll to see if she's still dry. "It's been a little while since Dolly used the potty, so we better check to see if she's still dry." Physically guide your child's hand to feel the doll's underpants. When she feels that they are still dry, celebrate just like you did when Dolly went pee-pee on the potty. Explain that this time you're celebrating because Dolly kept her big-kid pants dry. Repeat the same treat sequence you used when Dolly used the potty, again giving the doll's treat to the child if she agrees to "someday" keep her big-kid underpants dry.

I tell parents that they don't have to act like they're jacked up on four pots of coffee and a pound of sugar, but it helps. Seriously. The more excited you are and the more your voice and your movements show your enthusiasm, the more excited your child will be and the more he will want to go along with whatever you suggest. Excitement and enthusiasm are contagious.

After each book, potty video, or game, check the doll's underpants. When she stays dry, repeat the treat sequence and dialogue, and don't forget a sticker for Dolly's Potty Progress Chart.

ACCIDENTS

Plan for the doll to have eight or nine wetting accidents and two or three BM accidents before lunch. This is the point in the party to change the seating arrangement. Before now, the doll was sitting between you and your child. Now, so you can discreetly stage the doll's accidents and keep the mess on the waterproof blanket, sit next to your child and put the doll on your opposite side.

Begin with a bladder control accident. While your child is

preoccupied with a potty video or game, really saturate the doll's underpants. (As mentioned in chapter three, make sure you have at least a dozen big-kid underpants for your child and a dozen pairs for the doll.) Say something like, "Katharine, Dolly's such a big girl, let's feel if she's still dry." Guide the child's hand to feel the doll's underpants and when she feels that they are sopping wet, her eyes will spring open with surprise. Kids really react to the soaking wet underpants. Their little eyes pop out like cartoon characters'.

STUFFED TOYS MINUS THE MESS

If you decide to use a stuffed toy instead of a washable doll for your potty party, you'll want to modify my wetting accident instructions and BM suggestions (that is to say, mini prunes) so you don't permanently stain or damage the faux fur or fabric.

Some of the parents in my Potty-Training Boot Camps have successfully wrapped the toy's "bottom" with plastic wrap and then put underpants on top. If you don't think your child will buy this approach, try using brown clay shaped into the form of small BMs. If it's not too hot on your party day, you can also reshape Tootsie Rolls or use chocolate-covered peanuts. Obviously the key will be to remove them from the toy's underpants before they begin to melt. (And don't risk letting your child see you eat them! One of the dads in my class had that happen and it opened a whole new can of worms!)

For wetting accidents, take a wet sponge and when your child isn't looking, gently press it against the toy's underpants, just enough to make them damp.

With real concern in your voice, say something like, "Look what happened. Dolly went pee-pee in her underpants." Your child's facial expression will mirror your level of concern and she's likely to be very curious about what's going on. Continue by saying, "Oh my gosh! What do we do when we go pee-pee in our underpants? I think Dolly needs to practice. Let's take off her wet underpants and put her on the potty. Because if she goes and sits on the potty that's going to help her build potty-training memory muscles, and remember that we go pee-pee on the potty. We don't go pee-pee in our underpants."

Walk into the bathroom with your child and the doll and direct him to sit the doll on the potty-chair. Then ask your child, "How long do you think Dolly should sit on the potty so he remembers?" After a few minutes, ask, "Do you think Dolly has been practicing on the potty long enough?" Sometimes your child will say, "No, I think he needs to sit there a little longer." It's amazing to watch a toddler turn into a teacher! Wait another minute or so and then ask, "Do you think Dolly understands now? Can he get off the potty and play with us again now?" Once your child agrees, direct him to help you put clean underpants on the doll. "Let's go put some dry underpants on Dolly!" Lay the doll down and let your child help you tape the dry pair of big-kid underpants on the doll. (Kids love playing with tape, so they really like taping the big-kid underpants on the doll. You can also let them put a few stickers on top of the tape, or use character theme Band-Aids instead of tape.)

Once the clean underpants are on the doll, point to the doll and say, "Remember, Dolly. You're a big boy, so no more pee-pee in your pants!" Then get your child to join in and say it with you. Point to the doll and together with your child say, "No more pee-pee in your pants!"

Go back to the party room and play another game or read another book. After every one or two activities, lead your child to check if Dolly is still clean and dry. Each time the doll successfully stays dry, repeat the treat sequence and the dialogue, allowing your child to have the treat after he agrees to use the potty "someday" or "every time," and put a sticker on Dolly's Potty Progress Chart.

Now it's time for a BM accident. Put in a potty-training video and tell your child, "Let's show Dolly this video so she can see how other kids go potty." While your child is watching the video, secretly slip some baby food prunes or chocolate frosting into the doll's underpants. Then, when the video is over, start sniffing around as if you smell something odd. Get your child involved in the detective work. "Mary, do you smell something? I think I smell poopy." You can really have fun with this, and your toddler will probably really get in to it. Sniff under the couch, sniff the cat or the dog, and sniff your child. Ask, "Do you smell that?" You can even say, "I didn't go poopy in my pants. Did you go poopy in your pants?" And when she says no, you can say, "Oh my gosh, do you think that Dolly went poopy in her pants? We'd better investigate. Come on, Mary, let's look in Dolly's underpants."

When Mary discovers the poop, exclaim, "Oh my gosh, Dolly did go poopy in her pants. We don't go poopy in our pants, do we? Let's clean Dolly up and change her pants. I think Dolly forgot that big girls go poopy on the potty." Then ask your child, "What can we do to help Dolly remember to go poopy on the potty and not in her big-girl pants?" Eventually, you want your child to respond by saying that the doll should sit on the potty to practice to help her build her potty-training memory muscles, and also to remember to use the potty. But until your child supplies this response, fill in the blanks for her.

This is another opportunity to really exaggerate the idea of the doll pooping in her pants and in places other than on the potty. You can say, "We'd better get Dolly to the potty fast, or she might accidentally poop on the carpet next. Hurry up and put her on the potty before she poops on SpongeBob!" Most toddlers find this sort of humor very funny.

Help your child remove the doll's soiled underpants and guide her to wipe the doll with a wet wipe or toilet paper. Then tell her to put her doll on the potty-chair and ask her how long she thinks Dolly should sit there to practice and help her remember that big kids don't go poopy in their pants. Repeat the same dialogue that you had when the doll wet its big-kid underpants, allowing your child to decide when the doll can get off the potty.

BUILDING POTTY-TRAINING MEMORY MUSCLES

Each time you and your child discover that Dolly's underpants are wet or soiled, after you've asked the questions suggested in the accidents section, suggest, "Let's help Dolly build her potty-training memory muscles!" When you make that suggestion, *tap your temples.* Tapping your temples as you say the words creates a visual image to reinforce the verbal message. Explain to your child that after each accident, Dolly sits on the potty to build her potty-training memory muscles so she can remember that she doesn't have accidents in her underpants. She goes on the potty.

 ### YOU CAN SAY THAT AGAIN!

"Laughter is the shortest distance between two people."

—VICTOR BORGE

Once your child says the doll has had enough practice, direct her attention back to the party room for another game or activity. By now, it should be almost time for lunch and you want to end the morning on a high note, by having the doll successfully use the potty one more time.

Suggest that Dolly has to go pee-pee, and instruct your child to take the doll to the potty-chair. Once again, make the doll pee in the potty and celebrate its success just as you did the first time. Repeat the treat sequence and dialogue again and announce that you and your child will now have a party to celebrate Dolly becoming a big kid and throwing away her diapers!

LUNCHTIME

Lunchtime is a celebration of Dolly graduating from diapers to big-kid underpants. You are stressing the idea that babies wear diapers and Dolly isn't a baby anymore, so now she wears big-kid underpants, stays dry all day, and uses the potty. Give lots of attention to the doll so that your child understands that going on the potty is a big deal. Let your child know that "someday" or "every time" when he goes on the potty, he will have a Big Kid Celebration too. Some parents have party hats, noisemakers, horns, and even silly string for this festive celebration. Each theme party in chapter six offers suggestions for the doll's celebration party and for your toddler's Grand Finale Big Kid Celebration at the end of the day.

Since my son was crazy about Chuck E. Cheese, at lunch I had my brother call, posing as the giant mouse himself. Using a high-pitched mouse voice he congratulated Spencer for potty training the doll and told him, "Someday when you use the potty and wear big-kid pants, maybe you can come and celebrate with me!" That phone call proved to be a huge motivating force all afternoon!

NAPTIME

If your child is used to taking a nap after lunch, make sure he takes one today too. This is also a chance for you to kick back and catch your breath before the potty party afternoon where your child will be the one learning to use the potty.

Potty Party Afternoon

During this half of the party, you will be motivating your child to use the potty and to keep his pants dry. You will also be modeling using the potty, so it's important that you drink as much as your child. Both you and your child receive treats and praise for staying dry and for using the potty. And during the Grand Finale Big Kid Celebration at the end of the day, your child receives a few wrapped presents from you and your family, and you receive your wrapped present for being a potty pro extraordinaire!

The afternoon portion of the potty party is essentially a re-

YOU CAN SAY THAT AGAIN!

"Example is not the main thing in influencing others. It is the only thing."

—ALBERT SCHWEITZER

peat of the morning, but now you are focusing on the child, rather than the doll.

When the child wakes up from her nap say, "Guess who stayed dry the whole time you were taking your nap? Dolly! That's right. Yeah, Dolly is really remembering that he's a big boy! Let's give Dolly a treat and a sticker on his potty chart since he's such a big boy and he didn't go pee-pee in his underpants."

Then say, "Matthew, Dolly and I have a surprise for you!" Give him the wrapped present that contains the big-kid underwear that matches or is similar to the doll's underpants. Get really excited when he opens it and say, "Let's try on our big-boy underwear now!" Help him to put it on and within nanoseconds, before he has a chance to have an accident, have a dialogue about him being a big kid.

Draw attention to the big-boy pants and say, "Look Matthew, you're a big kid too! Your underpants are dry too!" Take his hands and place them up against his underpants so he can feel

EXPERTS SAY

Record. Record. Record.

"Before you begin your actual toilet training program, you need to know what your child's elimination pattern is. Give yourself two weeks to do nothing out of the ordinary except check your child's diaper—every hour—and record what you find. Knowing the answer—identifying your child's pattern—is at the core of successful training."

—ALAN BRIGHTMAN, PH.D., AUTHOR OF *STEPS TO INDEPENDENCE*

what dry means. Praise him, jump up and down, and get just as excited as you did when Dolly stayed dry. Give him a big hug and say, "You can have a treat now because you're a big kid just like Dolly!" Then run with him to the treat tray and let him pick out whatever he wants.

YOU DON'T SAY

"I bought toddler underwear and a potty seat that fit on our bathroom toilet before I started. For my daughter it was Lion King underwear and for my son it was Nemo underwear. The trick with the underwear was that my kids did not like seeing their favorite characters being wet."

—LISA MONROE

In the afternoon, you need to encourage your child to drink as much as possible to ensure potty success. Offer as many different drinks as your child likes. Every five or ten minutes hold the cup up to his lips and encourage drinking.

The more your child urinates during training, the more potty practice he'll get, so it's *very* important to encourage him to drink. And don't even think that milk and water are going to work—they're so not! In most cases, you are going to have to kick it up a notch with the beverages—splurge a bit. When my son was a toddler, I didn't give him anything but healthy, organic foods and drinks. But on potty party day, I pulled out all the stops. I bought two bags of treats and drinks that I thought he'd like. His potty party was the first day that he ever had M&Ms, and he went crazy for them! Just that one M&M that he got to eat each time on behalf of Dolly was a huge incentive for him.

To motivate your child to use the potty, use a lot of positive reinforcement: praise, hugs, and treats. You will give them *frequently,* very *enthusiastically,* and *immediately* after your child urinates in the potty and each time he checks his big-kid underpants and they are dry.

When he does have an accident, don't treat it as a bad thing. Simply say, "Everybody has accidents when we're learning and we all need to practice." Take his hand and while walking to the bathroom, say, "Mommy needs to practice too. Come with Mommy while I sit on the toilet and practice and you can sit on your potty and practice too. We can both sit here together."

If your child is using a seat adapter, sit on a chair or stool directly in front of him and say, "Let's both sit in the bathroom for practice, so we can keep each other company."

Reinforce the idea that having accidents is part of learning something new. Never criticize, tease, or reprimand your child for having an accident. Instead, reinforce the message of building potty-training memory muscles.

Potty Trips and Tips

A big part of the afternoon is spent going to the potty-chair and actually sitting in the chair. Make sure you have a big, bright Potty Progress Chart on the bathroom wall for your child. Put it up right next to the one you put up for the doll. You can let your child select a sticker for each time she pees on the potty, each time you check her pants and they are dry, each time she poops, and even when she tries or sits on the potty to practice after having an accident.

During the afternoon, you'll be leading your child to go to the potty, lower her pants, seat herself, sit for several minutes, then stand up again and pull up her pants. If she sits on the potty-chair for a few minutes on each try, she will eventually urinate while seated. When this happens, it's very important that you really whoop up the celebrating to show your child how proud and excited she has made you.

Make a Bladder Time Chart like the one on page 89 so you can keep track of how often your child has to urinate.

This varies widely from one child to another. If you're leading

DELICIOUS DRINKS

VERY CHERRY BERRY

½ cup frozen cherries
½ cup frozen raspberries
¾ cup raspberry sherbet
¾ cup apple juice

Mix in a blender.

PEACHY CREAM

1 cup orange sherbet
1 cup frozen peaches
¾ cup juice from canned peaches

Mix in blender.

KIWI LIME

2 lime frozen fruit bars
2 kiwis (scooped out of skin)
1 tablespoon cream of coconut

Break the bars from their sticks. Place all ingredients in a blender and mix well.

BERRY SMOOTH

½ cup frozen blackberries
1 cup frozen blueberries
½ cup vanilla yogurt
¼ cup grape juice
¼ cup milk

Blend well.

your child to the potty-chair every seven minutes and he doesn't have to go for twenty or thirty minutes, there's a greater chance of meeting with resistance. To help your child be successful, lead him to sit on the potty just a minute or two before you estimate that he'll really have to go.

Your goal is to have your child urinate on the potty at least four or five times over the course of the afternoon. To achieve that, you have to encourage your child to drink a lot of liquids. In addition to offering drinks that your child will love, consider using some crazy straws to entice your child to drink more.

To increase your child's potty-training success, give prompting at a moment she signals she has to go: crossing her legs, pacing, getting fidgety, holding her genitals, or whatever she normally does to indicate she has to urinate. When you see these signs, put your hand on her belly and ask, "Can you feel how your tummy feels right now? That means you have to use the potty." And then race to the potty-chair. After your child has urinated in the potty-chair and you've completed your celebration, teach her to remove the pot, empty it in the big toilet, flush the toilet, and

★ BLADDER TIME CHART ★										
POTTY PARTY DAY and TEN DAYS FOLLOWING										
	PARTY DAY	ONE	TWO	THREE	FOUR	FIVE	SIX	SEVEN	EIGHT	NINE	TEN
MORNING											
7											
8											
9											
10											
11											
AFTERNOON											
12											
1											
2											
3											
4											
5											
EVENING											
6											
7											
8											
9											

reinsert the pot into the chair. You will also want to teach your child how to wipe herself and wash her hands.

The two most common problems are lowering underwear and pants and not wanting to walk to the potty. Use yourself as a model to show your child how to go on the potty. Tell him, "See, Steven, I'm a big kid too. I go pee-pee on the potty." Give yourself a treat and a drink. Eventually your child will carry out these instructions with less prompting.

20/5/10 RULE FOR POTTY PRACTICE

 If your child does not show outward signs of needing to urinate (fidgeting, pacing, holding their genitals) and you can't determine a pattern with your bladder time chart, you will need to beat the odds by using the 20/5/10 rule for potty practice.

In every 20-minute period, give your child two 5-minute chances to go potty, with a 10-minute break in between. If nothing happens, reward her with a hug and sticker for trying, and go back to the party and repeat the process in 20-minute cycles. When she does urinate, ask her to describe the feeling she had just before she went. Together, you can learn to identify the warning signs.

While it would be great if your child has a bowel movement on the potty-chair during the potty party, you really can't count on this happening. But with enough liquids, you can count on her urinating at least a handful of times while sitting on the potty-chair.

Remember, never ask: Do you have to go pee-pee? Do you want to sit on the potty? Or any other question that can be answered with the word no. Remember that the no word is one of the most powerful weapons in a toddler's arsenal. Don't give her the chance to use it!

The dialogue sequence is: *Making a statement, then encouraging an action.*

For example: I think Dolly went pee-pee in her underpants. Let's feel her underpants to see if they are wet.

Or: Mommy has to go pee-pee in the potty. Race me to the bathroom!

Then race him into the bathroom and say, "Now you and Mommy get to sit on the potty like Dolly did, and then we both get to pick a special treat."

The trick is getting them on the potty and then getting them to sit there for a little while. In addition to the potty practice activities detailed in your theme party description, you can use flash cards of colors, shapes, objects, and animals to get them to relax and sit still for a few minutes. You can also let them draw a picture with an Etch A Sketch, or you can play I Spy. The secret is to have something fun and interesting to do each time that the child sits on the potty-chair. I have lots of suggestions for each party theme in the next chapter.

Just as you did with the doll, each time your child uses the potty and each time she is dry when you check her big-girl pants, she gets rewarded with

TIPS FOR TOILET PAPER CONTROL

Parents from Potty-Training Boot Camp have many suggestions for TP.

1. Put roll on backward so paper comes from the back rather than down from the front. Most children "slap" paper downward, not up. This helps control excess.

2. Some parents remove the TP completely from the holder, but keep it within the child's reach.

3. Other parents make it harder for a child to unroll it by squishing or misshaping the roll. It doesn't turn as easily and helps the child only take what is needed.

4. Place a rubber band around the roll if you have a child who uses TP as a source of entertainment while sitting on the potty.

5. Some parents use measuring games: roll the paper down to floor, have child use only four squares or a strip the length of the forearm.

Tips for larger/older child using adult toilet seat.

1. Hold child securely yourself, especially if you are in a public restroom.

2. Boy urinates while sitting down backward with legs straddling toilet with his little soldier pointing downward.

3. Girl: also straddle (forward/backward) seat sitting as far back as possible or sideways, always being careful to sink her bottom low enough to prevent urine from going through the seat ring and over the bowl rim onto the floor.

4. Both: in the beginning of potty training, it's best to remove underwear and pants to avoid wetting them.

FROM THE MOUTHS OF BABES

My recently potty trained daughter Jenna and I had just gotten out of the indoor swimming pool at our health club. As I was squatting down to dry her off, my swimsuit started dripping water onto the floor. Jenna gasped, pointed at the growing puddle, and said, "Mommy, we don't go pee-pee on the floor!"

praise and a treat or a prize and a sticker for her potty chart. Use a list of people that your child really likes and tell her how happy everyone is that she goes on the potty. For example, "Liza, you do a great job of sitting on the potty like Grandma." "Doug is a big boy just like Daddy." "Your pants are dry just like Chuck E. Cheese."

At the end of the potty training party, stage the Grand Finale Big Kid Celebration. This is where you either take the party on the road, or invite family and friends to come to the house to celebrate your child's success. The secret is to plan festivities that your child will really enjoy.

A very important part of the Big Kid Celebration is letting your child throw away her diapers. Have her toss them into a clean trash bag (that way you can actually donate them to a charity or use them as portable potty stuffing for road trips). Stress the idea that babies wear diapers and big kids wear underpants (and sometimes pull-ups). When your child throws away the diapers a resounding cheer should go up from every-

GRANDMA SAYS

There's a fine line between positive reinforcement and bribery.

one in the room, followed by joyful dancing, hugging, and lots of congratulating!

During the celebration, reinforce your child's potty-training experience by leading her to practice and to teach others. You might say, "Sarah, show Daddy where the potty is," or "Billy, we should show Daddy how to go potty because everybody needs to practice going pee-pee on the potty."

One final note for party day is that this training is for daytime only. Nighttime dryness will come in time. Until then, use disposable pull-ups at night, while you're out and about, and while your child is napping.

When you use disposable pull-ups, refer to them as disposable big-kid underpants. Stress that your child is wearing them *just in case*. And never put another diaper on your child because, if you do, you'll be sending a very mixed message. A few weeks after my son's potty party, he was staying dry on some nights but not all nights, so he was still wearing disposable pull-ups at night. One night at about 9 P.M. I realized that I was out of pull-ups, so I tried to sneak a diaper onto my son. He absolutely wouldn't let me do it. He said, "No, no, no. I'm a big boy. I'm not a baby," and I literally had to drive to the store and pick up a bag of pull-ups.

With the basics of potty training complete, now we need to move on to the potty parties!

6. potty party plans and themes

In raising my children,
I have lost my mind but found my soul.

—LISA T. SHEPHERD

Playing is one of the best ways for young children to learn. When the educational playtime engages a variety of senses—sight, hearing, touch, taste, and scent—toddlers tend to learn new concepts and skills both better and faster. And, as icing on the cake, they also discover that learning is fun!

Although in an earlier chapter I lamented (only partially tongue-in-cheek) about toilet training coinciding with the terrible twos, there's actually an upside to this timing. Children between two and three and a half years old have ripe imaginations, love to have fun, and are thrilled to have their parents' attention and praise. Regardless of how many times they say no in an hour, they ultimately want to please you and need to know that you're proud of them. The One-Day Potty-Training Party is designed to cater to the minds and hearts of kids at this age.

All potty parties use the same teaching methods, modeling, and hands-on experience and the basic framework for all par-

DID YOU KNOW?

22 percent of kids are out of diapers by age 2.5
60 percent are out of diapers by age 3
88 percent are out of diapers by age 3.5

ties is the same. (This chapter will walk you through the entire potty party sequence.) By incorporating theme decorations, activities, and treats into the basic framework, you make the learning process exciting, stimulating, and very rewarding. All themes include the following:

Decorations for party room and bathroom

Drinks

Activities

Edible and play treats

Books and videos

Presents and prizes

Shopping lists

If the thought of planning a party raises your stress level, remember that to a toddler the word "party," loosely translated, just means *fun*. The most important part of the learning process is making it a positive experience. Your child will be so excited to have your undivided attention that a few bows and balloons will be enough to show that today is a party day and to help declare that today, something special is happening!

For those of you who really get into party planning and decorating, there are a handful of easy ideas for each theme. You can also mix and match decorations, treats, activities, games, and prizes from different parties. And remember, your enthusiasm and excitement will play a larger part in encouraging your child to learn to use the potty than all the presents, prizes, treats, or decorations in the world.

GRANDMA SAYS

If you don't have enough patience to keep a sense of humor when you're potty training your child, it's best to behave as if you do.

A Word About the Treats Tray

The Treats Tray holds bite-size edible treats, such as marshmallows, and small play treats, like a miniature container of modeling clay. The treats are used in concert with your praise and a dialogue sequence that reinforces your child's willingness to use the potty. Each party theme offers suggestions for the Treats Tray and all of them have several healthy edible treat options.

During the morning of the party you select the treats for the doll and then offer them to your child, so you have total control over what your child ends up eating. During the afternoon, you allow your child to choose her own treats. Even if she makes unhealthy choices all afternoon, the amount of sweets or salty snacks she consumes will still be less than a cup or so, total.

Buy miniature paper party cups (the tiny ones that only hold about 2 ounces). Each edible treat fits in the cup, so every snack is only a bite or two. You can also put decorative stickers on the snack cups.

Keep in mind that the sincere and enthusiastic praise you give to your child will mean much more than a treat, so make your praise the most exciting part of your interaction. The treat is simply a tangible reward to help your child associate learning with pleasure.

EXPERTS SAY

The strongest motivation for an independently minded child to become toilet trained is the feeling of being more grown up.

TREATS TRAY TIP

For a sturdy, convenient, and washable Treats Tray, use a muffin or cupcake tin decorated with ribbons, bows, and theme stickers.

Potty Practice

Two of the secrets to making the potty party a success are being able to get your child to the potty when she has to go and keeping her on the seat long enough for the blessed event to occur.

POTTY PARTY TREAT BOX

Contrary to popular belief, healthy treats can be tasty! Visit your local health food or organic food store. You can also order a goodie box from The Web of Life at www.weboflifewestlake.com or by calling 440-899-2882. The goodie box treats are organic and have high fiber and no cholesterol, hydrogenated oils, trans fats, or preservatives.

For this reason, every theme party offers helpful suggestions for fun ways to get children into the bathroom with a few activities that you can do with your child when he is sitting on the potty. The following is a list of activities that will work for all parties.

To the Potty!

Here are some fun ways to get your child into the bathroom:

RHYTHM AND SHOES

Clap each time your child takes a step, keeping in time with her rhythm. Encourage your child to run, hop, jump, gallop, and skip . . . and continue to clap out the rhythm her feet make. For a change, have your child clap out stepping rhythms that you make. Be sure they are reasonably slow and simple.

SPAGHETTI DANCE

Lie on the floor, side by side. Your bodies should be stiff and straight like uncooked spaghetti. The only way you can move is to roll. That is, until you're cooked! Now, pretend you are being boiled. Twist and swirl your bodies the way spaghetti moves while it's cooking. Imagine you are being drained in a colander and then tossed with olive oil, butter, or sauce.

SILLY STEPS

Encourage your child to make up silly ways of walking. The sillier the better! You try it too. Can he do his silly walks backward or sideways? Can you?

AWARD-WINNING ADVICE

 My daughter Ellie wasn't into potty charts or stickers, but she loved *The Wizard of Oz*. So we made a yellow brick road out of pieces of construction paper that led from her bedroom down the hall to the bathroom. Each time she used her potty-chair, I gave her a page from a *Wizard of Oz* coloring book. As soon as she colored the picture, we taped it on one of the yellow bricks beginning with the one outside her bedroom door. By the time all the bricks had colored pictures taped on them, Ellie was successfully potty trained. Her reward for making it all the way to Oz was her own copy of *The Wizard of Oz* DVD.

POOPA RACHA DANCE

Partly fill two long-necked plastic bottles with rice, beans, bird-seed, or macaroni. Seal the bottle with masking tape or bottle lids. Wrap additional tape around the neck to make a comfortable handle. Then use the bottles as maracas and dance to the bathroom!

Potty Fun

These are fun ways to pass the time while your child is on the potty.

GUESSING GAMES

FEELS LIKE

Without your child watching, place three or four of her small toys inside a pillowcase and tie the end shut with a rubber band. Challenge her to guess what the toys are, just by feeling them.

20 QUESTIONS

Think of an object your child is familiar with. Have him try to guess the object by asking up to twenty questions. Exchange roles.

WORD GAMES

RHYME TIME

Say a word and have your child say a word that rhymes with it. For example, you might say "Flush," and your child might say "Mush."

OPPOSITES

Say a word like "hot" and have your child say the opposite word—like "cold."

CREATE A STORY

Make up the first few sentences of a story and then encourage your child to make up the next couple of sentences. Go back and forth until you both decide the story is finished.

SOUNDS LIKE?

Use your voice to imitate everyday sounds. Try imitating sounds like a door shutting, telephone ringing, washing machine, teakettle whistling, fire crackling. (Do indoor and outdoor sounds.)

WHY I LOVE YOU!

Take turns telling each other all the reasons you love them or they make you happy.

MOTION GAMES

COPY CATS

Set a small stool across from your child's potty-chair or sit on the floor so you can be eye to eye. Pretend that your child is a mirror and must do whatever you do. Start with slow, simple movements that you know your child can follow. After a few minutes, it's your turn to be the mirror.

HAND TALK

Together with your child, make up three or four hand signals to communicate silent messages. Keep it simple. For example, placing your hands over your heart could mean "I love you." Putting your two palms together could be the signal for "Thank you." Holding up one finger might mean "I have to pee."

DUELING BUBBLES

Blow bubbles at your child and have him blow them back at you. You can also blow bubbles at the same time and try to either hit or avoid each other's bubbles.

MUSICAL GAMES

OPERA STARS

Instead of talking to each other, just sing. The quality of the singing isn't important. The important thing is to sing every word.

SING ALONG

Sing songs with your child (with or without musical accompaniment like a CD or tape). Let her choose the songs she wants to sing and if she runs out of ideas, try some old classics like "On Top of Spaghetti, All Covered with Cheese," "Old MacDonald Had a Farm," and "Bingo."

POTTY LYRICS

You can also change the words to songs that your child already knows. For example, instead of singing "The wheels on the bus go round and round" change the words to, "This is how we flush, flush, flush," "Wash our hands, wash our hands," "Wipe ourselves, wipe ourselves," "Pull up our pants, pull up our pants," etc.

Fun Gifts and Gadgets That Work with All Potty Parties

EMMA AND PAUL TOILET-TRAINING DOLLS

Since its founding, Corolle has achieved global recognition for its dolls, winning more that thirty international awards for design and play excellence. They're vanilla scented, which kids love (and parents too). And the dolls have the most incredibly soft, supple skin. An added bonus, if you're training a boy, is that Paul is anatomically correct!

www.corolledolls.com

800-668-4846

TP SAVER

The TP Saver prevents the unrolling of toilet paper by babies, toddlers, and pets. The TP Saver is perfect for toilet training, giving you control over the paper or allowing metered use. www.inventiveparent.com

FLUSHIN' FRIENDS

Decorative toilet handle covers in safari characters encourage children to flush. www.parentsofinvention.com

OCTODOG'S FRANKFURTER CONVERTER

This gadget turns a hot dog into an octopus. www.octodog.net

THE PETER POTTY

The Peter Potty is the world's only flushable and adjustable toddler urinal. (No plumbing required!) What a great tool to use during the maintenance phase.

www.peterpotty.com

312-997-2310

POTTY BENCH BY BOON

The Potty Bench by Boon is a training potty featuring two enclosed side storage spaces for organizing potty training supplies, and a pull-out drawer for easy sanitary clean-up. Simply close the lid to use as a large, sturdy stool that holds up to 300 pounds. The sleek, modern design includes a built-in toilet paper holder and a removable soft deflector shield.

www.booninc.com

888-376-4763

POTTIESTICKERS

This is a very innovative potty-training reward system. A winner of numerous awards, including Best New Product at the American Business Awards, judged by Donald Trump. With twelve designs and a downloadable certificate. You can tailor them to nearly all the theme parties.

www.pottiestickers.com

866-219-3474

THEY'LL EAT YOUR WORDS

M&Ms can personalize your potty message and theme color with "way to go," "great job," or other encouraging words.

www.mms.com

880-696-6788

Phrases That Pay

Phrases That Pay are statements you can make and questions you can ask to facilitate the toilet-training process.

Because many children are particularly sensitive about having accidents or making mistakes during toilet training, it's very important for parents to direct all reprimands at the potty-training doll or stuffed animal and none of them at your child. Interacting with the doll is also a good way to reinforce a message without overstating the point.

GRANDMA SAYS

When a young child says he has to go potty, he means "Now."

GETTING YOUR CHILD INTO THE BATHROOM

Let's be honest, getting your child into the bathroom is not an easy feat. Most children are not enthusiastic about *walking* into the bathroom and *trying* to use the potty. Rarely, if ever, will asking the question "Do you need to use the potty?" work. Instead, when you want them to go to the bathroom or you notice that they are fidgeting, holding their genitals, crossing their legs, or pacing, use the *suggestion/command* technique.

"Mommy has to use the bathroom. Let's look at some books together and keep each other company."

"Dolly really looks like she has to use the potty. Do you want to show her or should I? Let's put Dolly on the big toilet and you can sit on the potty and we can all sing songs until Dolly goes pee-pee."

"Wow, Dolly is becoming such a big kid! After we all go potty, let's tell Dolly he can try flushing the toilet all by himself. We can all sing a little song about waving bye-bye to the pee-pee and poopy after he flushes. Let's give it a try."

FROM THE MOUTHS OF BABES

 My three-year-old daughter Elise's preschool teacher often tells the children in her class to turn on their listening ears when she has something important she needs to tell them. The kids respond to this command by reaching up and gently squeezing their earlobes. One night when Elise was pretending not to hear my request that she use her potty-chair before going to bed, I asked her, "Honey, do you have on your listening ears?" She tilted her head, considered the question for a few seconds, and then said, "Yes, but the batteries are dead."

GENERAL POTTY DIALOGUE WITH DOLLY

While you are in the midst of your potty party and during the maintenance phase, you will want to encourage dialogue about the importance of staying dry, the basic function of the potty-chair, and all the people who are proud of your child for staying dry.

After you make your prompting remarks, don't wait around to hear a possible no. Take off hopping, skipping, or racing down the hall. Make a game out of it.

"It's been a while since Dolly used the potty. Let's take him into the bathroom and show him how big kids use their potty-chair."

"Let's allow Dolly to use the *other* bathroom in our house so she can practice using her potty-chair in different places. Together we can show Dolly how using different toilets is really fun. I'll sit on my toilet and you can sit on your potty and all three of us will play I Spy."

"I have been saving some special books to read to you and Dolly in the bathroom. Let's all hop to the bathroom and see who can hop there first."

"Let's show Daddy what big kids we are for all going to the bathroom together."

"I bet Grandma and Granddad would be really happy to know you're a big kid. Let's show them how you can go pee-pee in the potty all by yourself."

"The next time we all try to use the potty, let's play some games. Do you think Dolly would like to play Opposites or 20 Questions? Let's all race to the bathroom and whoever wins can pick the game to play."

POTTY-TRAINING BOOT CAMP TIP

On a poster board on the inside of the bathroom door, I taped up photos of my son's (same-aged) cousins using their potty-chairs. Seeing the photos and knowing that his cousins were "big kids" helped motivate my son to learn.

DOLL DIALOGUE TO ENCOURAGE BOWEL MOVEMENTS

Some children are reluctant to have their bowel movements on the potty and prefer to go off and hide. Such hiding behavior is very common during toilet training. A lot of parents in my boot camps shared stories of the children requesting a diaper and then running off to poop in a private place. If this is what your child does, you will want to encourage a lot of conversation with the doll on this topic. The good news is that the final stage of toilet mastery isn't too far away.

"Did you notice Dolly keeps pooping in his diaper? He keeps going off and hiding whenever he needs to poop. Let's both tell Dolly together, Dolly, no more poopies in your pants." (Say this as you both wave a finger at Dolly gesturing no.)

"I think Dolly keeps forgetting where big kids go to poop. I think Dolly should practice walking to and sitting on the potty for a few minutes. This will help her build her potty-training

---

FROM THE MOUTHS OF BABES

While my son John was learning to use the potty, one of his rewards for successfully using his potty-chair was calling his father to report the good news. One morning after John had a BM he ran to the phone to call Dad. I knew my husband Mike was in a meeting that morning, so I pushed the speed dial key for his voicemail and handed the phone to my son. My husband had an office full of clients when my son's voice suddenly boomed over the speaker phone, "Daddy! I pooped!" I had mistakenly pushed the direct dial key for my husband's office.

memory muscles. Let's go together with Dolly and put her on the potty."

"For some reason Dolly will make pee-pee on the potty, but poop only in his underwear. Let's tell Dolly that the next time he thinks he's ready to go poop to tell us and we'll help him on the potty. Let's tell him how proud we are of him because having clean underwear feels so good!"

POTTY DIALOGUE WHILE TRAVELING WITH DOLLY

If you're traveling, doll play can help your child learn to try new toilets. To ensure potty success on the road, a lot of parents try to take the fear out of a new potty experience by making it fun. For example, try singing a favorite nursery rhyme together or make up your own tune. My son and I used to sing "The pee in the potty goes flush, flush, flush," to the tune of "The Wheels on the Bus."

> **FREE POTTY-TRAINING eKIT**
>
> Huggies will send you a PULL-UPS Potty Training eKit—customized just for you and your Big Kid! Just take a few moments to answer the online quiz to reveal your child's potty-training style. It's a short, easy quiz and the eKit contains tools, activities, and expertise from moms and other experts.

"We've been in the car a long time. We better make sure Dolly uses the potty. Let's both show Dolly how we use a toilet in a public restroom."

"Dolly is really being a good kid for keeping his pants dry while we've been traveling. But let's make sure we take a potty break soon for Dolly. He'll think it's fun to use somebody else's toilet."

DOLL DIALOGUE TO ENCOURAGE NIGHTTIME DRYNESS

Dialogue with the doll or stuffed toy can also be used to reinforce staying dry at night.

"It makes me so happy that Dolly has been wearing her big-girl pants ever since our potty party and only needs to wear her *just in case* pants at night."

OUR POTTY PICNIC

"After taking Teri's class I was so excited to plan a potty-training day. The first thing I did was choose a theme. My daughter Natalie loves to eat outside. Picnic lunches and dinners are her ultimate favorites, so I chose to do a Potty Picnic indoors. I was careful to plan each aspect of the day according to this theme and her preferences.

"I put all of our food and treats in a picnic basket and a cooler. I also had plenty of wet paper towels and napkins on hand for clean up. In a separate picnic basket I individually wrapped many gifts—underpants and stickers in her favorite characters, training pants and rubber pants. I also wrapped Dolly and her bottle.

"When it was time to use the potty we had a potty parade. I had a variety of noise/musicmakers in a box. She would pick up one or two and proceed to the potty singing and dancing as she went. I would grab an instrument and join her.

"When Cinderella was on the potty we did many things, such as reading, singing, and blowing bubbles. She would try to blow the bubbles back at me, which helped her to relax and fill the potty. We had a very successful day."

—Michele Lungo

"Tonight while we're putting Dolly to bed, let's remind him that he should think about waking up all dry."

"Dolly has been staying dry for many nights in a row. Let's tell Dolly that she is becoming a big girl and she won't need to wear her just in case pants tonight."

Choosing a Fun Theme for Your Child

For the greatest success and the most enjoyable learning environment, select the theme party that is most compatible with your child's personality, energy level, and preferences. It's important for you to like the theme too, but your personal favorite isn't necessarily the best choice for your child.

The following quiz will help you hone in on the themes that are likely to be the best fits for your child.

Potty Party Pop Quiz ★★★★★★

My child tends to be:

A. Very active

B. Active

C. Somewhat active

Among the following, my child would most frequently choose

A. Playing a sport, running, or dancing

B. Making a craft project or baking

C. Coloring, reading, or playing a board game

My child's favorite books and movies are

A. Action adventures

B. Animal or nature stories

C. Cartoons or magical fantasies

My child's favorite role-playing games tend to involve

A. Saving the day and/or being in the limelight

B. Adventures with friends (people, dolls, and animals)

C. Cartoon characters and/or magic and imagination

If you answered "A" the most, the following parties are likely to appeal most to your child:

A

Super Hero Saves the Day
Celebrity Star Salute
Seriously Silly Circus
Knights of the Round Table

If you have mostly "B" answers, your child will probably enjoy the following parties:

B

Fun on the Farm
Incredibly Cool Camp Out
Splish Splash Beach Bash
All Aboard Train Trip

If you have mostly "C" answers, your child will most likely have fun at the following parties:

C

Magic Carpet Express
Cartoon Character Carnival
Teddy Bear Picnic
The Princess Ball

CHILDREN WITH SPECIAL NEEDS

Contributed by Alan Brightman, Ph.D.,
Founder, Worldwide Disability Solutions Group,
   Apple Computer

For children with special needs, it's likely that the approach described in these pages will need to be substantially modified or, in fact, changed altogether. Indeed, if you are the parent of a child with developmental disabilities or with physical and/or sensory limitations, this is hardly news. You already know that for your child to learn most skills—including toilet training—it is critical that the teaching be tailored to meet his or her unique needs and capabilities.

For your child, one general teaching strategy will probably not work. Your child needs a strategy designed just for him or her.

While we don't have the space here to describe the particular kinds of tailoring you'll need to do for your child, we can offer you six general guidelines that we've learned from hundreds of parents of children with special needs. For more specific information on developing a specific approach to toilet training your child, we encourage you to take a look at the book listed at the end of this sidebar.

1. It's necessary, not fun.

Lucky (and rare) is the mother of any child with special needs who's had an easy time with toilet training. It's just not one of those thrilling parts of being a parent. It's time consuming. Labor intensive. Repetitive. And too often frustrating. What keeps the successful parents from putting up with all this, though, is simple: the end more than justifies the means. Whenever you can help your child become more independent in *any* area, the benefits to him and to you are obvious. With toilet training, the benefits may be most obvious of all.

So our message here is simple: persevere. Stay with it. You might have to make little changes along the way, but don't give up. You can't imagine how proud and happy (and, pardon the pun, relieved) you'll feel when you eventually succeed.

2. Be careful. Experts are everywhere.

Parents who have toilet trained their child know that their way works best. At least as far as *their* child is concerned. Naturally the successful parents are only too happy to share their expertise with you. Keep in mind, though, that your child isn't their child. And your house isn't their house. What worked for them may not work for you.

Remember that once you've developed the plan that you feel is best suited to your child, that's the plan you should follow consistently. *Your* plan for *your* child. Modify it when you must, but don't veer too far away from it. Otherwise you won't really have a plan at all. You'll just have a series of unconnected hunches. And we've yet to hear of any child who's followed the "hunch route" to success.

3. It's not just toilet training.

No doubt you know this already, but it bears a brief repeating: toilet training isn't just one skill. In fact it's closer to a dozen skills, all performed in a correct sequence. These are the individual skills: 1. Recognizing the need to go; 2. Waiting to eliminate; 3. Entering the bathroom; 4. Pulling pants down; 5. Sitting on the toilet; 6. Eliminating in the toilet; 7. Using toilet paper correctly; 8. Pulling pants back up; 9. Flushing the toilet; 10. Washing hands; 11. Drying hands.

No wonder toilet training takes time. That's a lot of skills to teach for just one behavior. But that's the point. Toilet training isn't just one behavior. It's a sequence of separate steps.

And even if your child already knows some of them, she or he won't be successfully toilet trained until she or he performs all of them in the correct order.

4. Ready or not?

There's a reason we don't try to toilet train infants. We can't! Infants don't have the necessary muscle control. It's physically impossible for them to be trained. The infant simply isn't ready.

Your child, too, may not be ready if she or he can't perform two necessary skills: 1. Follow simple instructions ("Come here, Billy."); and 2. Sitting in a chair for five minutes. If your child hasn't yet mastered these two skills, then you should work on teaching them first. Part of successful toilet training, after all, is stacking the cards in favor of success. If your child isn't able to follow simple instructions or sit for five minutes, then you don't yet have the necessary cards to stack.

5. Record. Record. Record.

Before you begin your actual toilet training program, you need to know what your child's elimination pattern is. When, in other words, is she or he most likely to wet or soil his pants? You can't officially start toilet training your child until you know the answer. And knowing the answer—identifying your child's pattern—is at the core of successful training.

We suggest that you give yourself two weeks to do nothing out of the ordinary except check your child's diaper—every hour—and record what you find. Start when your child wakes up in the morning and stay with it throughout the day. Whenever you find that the diaper is wet or soiled (even a little), be sure to change it. This way you'll be certain about whether there's been any activity

(continued)

in the following hour, and your child will get more used to being dry.

After two weeks sit down with your records and find your child's pattern. This is the pattern you'll use to determine your toilet-training schedule.

6. Long story short. Real short.

When your child is sitting on the toilet, she or he is there for a reason. And it's not social. So while you certainly want to be encouraging, you don't want to be a distraction.

Talk as little as you can. Be as matter-of-fact as you can.

When your child's through—whether or not she or he has been successful—and you've left the bathroom, feel free to praise as much as you want. But while he's doing his job, be sure to do yours. And with special needs children, yours involves being as nondistracting as you can be.

There you have it, a half dozen things to think about before you begin to toilet train your child with special needs. We urge you now to read the chapter about toilet-training techniques that you can find in *Steps to Independence: Teaching Everyday Skills to Children with Special Needs,* by Bruce Baker and Alan Brightman, published by Brookes Publishing.

Theme 1

Magic Carpet Express

Grab your wand and hitch a ride on the Magic Carpet Express. Fly away to Imagination Station, where wishes and make-believe are part of everyday life and nobody ever has a bad day. Cast spells that rhyme, fast-forward time, and turn a bad guy into slime. Theme colors are jewel tones such as rich reds, blues, golds, and teals.

DECORATIONS

Party Room: The Magic Room

Magic Carpet*

Paint a floor cloth (made out of natural canvas and coated with polyurethane) to look like a magic carpet. It can be used in the party room, the bathroom, and throughout the house. Leaks and spills can be wiped right off.

* Decorating tip from Matt and Shari of *Room by Room* on HGTV

Balloon Clouds

Buy a handful of colorful helium balloons and tie them to ribbons ranging from four feet to six feet in length. Use tape or low-tack putty to attach the balloon ribbons to the floor. You can also tie the balloons to pieces of furniture throughout the room.

Magic Hat Trick

Prepare this decoration ahead of time and hide it for the Grand Finale Big Kid Celebration. It will create a dramatic and lasting impression.

Use a costume or strong decorative magician's hat, top hat, or any hat that can be turned upside down and filled with marbles.

4–6 sheets of newspaper or tissue paper

2–4 cups of marbles

4–6 sparkler sticks

> Stuff the bottom half of the hat with newspaper or tissue paper.
>
> Fill the top half of the hat (to about one-inch below the brim) with marbles.
>
> Insert sparklers into the marbles and store out of sight.
>
> At the Grand Finale, light the sparklers as everyone enthusiastically cheers for your child and congratulates him for being a big kid.

Imagination Station: Bathroom Decorations

The Imagination Station decorating ideas were generously contributed by Matt and Shari of *Room by Room* on HGTV. Check out their website at: www.mattandshari.com.

Open Sesame

Wrap or cover the bathroom door with bright colored paper, as people do to their front doors at the holidays.

Imagination Station

Using cardboard or poster board, make a sign declaring the bathroom Imagination Station. Hang the sign at your child's eye level. You can hang the sign with ribbon attached to the top edge of the door with tacks.

Rainbow Ribbons

Tie long ribbons to the shower curtain rings. Make the ribbons long enough to reach the bathtub rim or within two or three feet of the floor.

Flying Streamers

For an exciting and dramatic effect, use low-tack putty to hang lots of streamers from the ceiling.

Night Sky or Select Scene

Paint an inexpensive shower curtain with fabric paints. Use stencils to paint shapes like stars, suns, and moons.

Fairy Dust

Sprinkle star confetti on the bathroom counter.

Magic Mirror

Using watercolor paints, paint your child's name on the top of the bathroom mirror. Add some theme stickers, ribbons, and bows to turn it into a playful Magic Mirror.

Magic Trunk and Contents

The Magic Trunk can be very small, very big, or somewhere in between. If your child will get an added thrill out of being able to sit or stand inside the box, consider picking up a large box at a U-Haul store or salvaging one from a neighbor or local store.

The idea is to get a cardboard box that you can wrap, paint, or decorate. The contents of the Magic Trunk can be purchased, made, improvised, or imagined.

Magic Wand

Buy a plastic or acrylic toy wand or make a wand out of a long-handled wooden or plastic spoon. Paint the spoon or wrap it with aluminum foil. Tie colorful ribbons to the handle of the spoon and use the spoon end as the handle.

Spell Book

Buy a small spiral notebook (3.5 × 5.5 inches or smaller) so your child has a place to draw pictures and attach new stickers.

Crazy Straws

Hide one or two of these fun straws for the afternoon. You will want to use every healthy means of encouraging your child to drink liquids.

Binoculars

Toy binoculars or make-believe binoculars for playing I Spy.

Water Soluble Packing Peanuts

The kind that melt when you wet them.

Magic Sponges

Biodegradable (flushable) miniature sponges that expand into shapes when they're wet. (See Resources.)

TREATS TRAY

Drinks

Bubbling Brew

¼ cup carbonated water, mineral water, or clear soda
¾ cup fruit juice

Your child gets to add ¼ cup carbonated water or clear soda, like Sprite, to fruit juice and say the magic words to make it fizz. Then your child can drink it while making a wish.

Milk Magic

Start with white milk, soymilk, or rice milk, and let your child add powder or syrup to turn it into chocolate or strawberry. If their Magic Wand is washable, they can use it to stir their concoction.

Wish Potion

Soda Sip
1 or 2 ounces of soda measured out into a miniature cup. Your child can make a wish as she drinks the wish potion.

Pop Up

2 ounces prune juice
1 ounce of cola

Mix well. Great for kids who tend to be constipated.

Edible Treats

Melting Ms: one or two M&Ms

Flying Fish: one or two fish-shaped crackers

Fairy Wands: one or two mini pretzel sticks

Fairy Wings: two potato chips

Magic Kiss: one Hershey's Kiss in silver foil wrap

Peanut Power: 1-inch piece of celery filled with peanut butter

Vanishing Apple Sauce: Let your child sprinkle a tiny bit of cinnamon on top of ¼ cup applesauce. Then say abracadabra and make the applesauce disappear by eating it!

Mystery Melon: one or two mini slices or cubes of a melon in season

Wrap some of the treat cups with tissue paper and tie them with a ribbon bow. Your child can wave her Magic Wand and turn the hidden treat into something guaranteed to be yummy or fun to play with! If you don't want your child to eat treats made with refined sugar, check out the alternatives available in health food stores.

Play Treats

All of these treats can be used during afternoon potty practice to help your child relax while sitting on the potty. Use the treats to keep your child engaged so she is willing to sit on the potty for several minutes at a time, too.

Magic Clay: Mini container of modeling clay.

Charming Bubbles: Mini container of bubbles with a bubble wand. Bubbles are a great activity for your child while sitting on her pottychair.

Super Stickers: A few new stickers that your child can put on her Potty Progress Chart or in her Spell Book.

Magic Sponges: Biodegradable (flushable) miniature sponges that expand into shapes when they're wet. (See Resources.)

ACTIVITIES

Alternate between the activities listed below, the theme party books, and the potty-training books and videos.

Morning

Coloring the Clouds

2 cups powdered sugar
¼ cup milk (or soy or rice milk)
Food coloring: red, blue, and yellow
Oyster crackers

First, mix the powdered sugar and the milk together in a medium-size bowl.

Divide the mixture into six small bowls.

Add red food coloring to one bowl, blue to another, and yellow to the third. Using the combinations below, you can create more colors for the remaining bowls.

1 squirt red + 1 squirt yellow = orange
1 squirt red + 1 squirt blue = purple
1 squirt blue + 1 squirt yellow = green

Dip the oyster cracker clouds into the different color mixtures and use them to make more treat cups. Eating a few as you go can be fun too.

Fast-Forward Time

Using a no-bake cookie mix, help your child mix the ingredients together and spread into a pan.

Put the pan in the oven and close the door. (Do not turn the oven on.) Have your child say the magic word "Abracadabra!" Open the oven. Take out the cookie tray with potholders and exclaim, "They're finished! Yay! Let's taste them and then put them on the counter for Dolly's Big Kid Party."

Afternoon

Potty Practice Activities

All of the following activities are designed to help make your child's experience of sitting on the potty-chair both fun and positive.

Cast a Spell That Rhymes

To make the pee disappear,
Just say the magic word: Flush!
And presto, the water is clear.

Turn a Bad Guy into Slime

Have your child draw "bad guy" faces on water-soluble packing peanuts. The peanuts are dropped into the potty and peed on, which turns them into "slime." If your child might have a negative reaction to the idea of bad guys or turning them into slime, encourage her to draw shapes and decorations on the peanuts instead.

I Spy

Play I Spy with binoculars. You can use the toy version or make-believe, by forming circles with your index fingers and thumbs and looking through them.

Simon Says

Whatever Simon says goes. Take turns with your child being Simon. Simon will give commands such as "stand on one foot," "rub your belly," etc. If Simon starts the sentence by saying Simon says, then you have to do it. If he doesn't begin by saying Simon says, then you don't do it. As soon as one of you is tricked, you change roles or switch to a different activity.

Theme Books

In addition to the potty training books listed in the Resources:

Which Would You Rather Be? by William Steig
When a crafty rabbit meets up with two inquisitive children, he reaches into his magic hat and pulls out the answers to a very important question: "Which would you rather be?"
Milo's Hat Trick by Jon Agee

Milo the Magnificent needs a clever new trick or he may never perform again.

Momma's Magical Purse by Paulette Bogan

A little boy doubts that his momma's purse is magical until trouble erupts at a rainy picnic.

Sylvester and the Magic Pebble by William Steig

A story about a donkey named Sylvester and the magic pebble that makes his dream come true.

The Magic Toolbox by Mie Araki

Fred the rhinoceros and Lulu the rabbit have a lot of fun building with their new toolbox.

SHOPPING LISTS

Party Room Decorations—The Magic Room

Magic Carpet

Natural canvas floor cloth

Paint (pick a background color and then pick one or two different colors for symbols and accents on the carpet)

Polyurethane

Paintbrushes

Balloon Clouds

6–12 colorful helium-filled balloons

Ribbon (cut into lengths ranging from 4 feet to 6 feet)

Masking tape or low-tack putty

Magic Hat Trick

Magician's Hat (top hat or any hat that can be turned upside-down and filled with marbles)

4–6 sheets of newspaper or tissue paper

2–4 cups of marbles

4–6 sparkler sticks

Bathroom (Imagination Station) Decorations

Open Sesame

Wrapping paper to cover the   Paint
    bathroom door   Paintbrushes

Imagination Station

Cardboard or poster board   Ribbon
Paint and paintbrush or   2 Tacks
    color marker

Rainbow Ribbons

Red, teal, blue, and gold ribbons

Flying Streamers

Multicolor streamers   Low-tack putty

Night Sky or Select Scene

Shower curtain   Paintbrushes
Fabric paints   Stencils of stars, suns, moons

Fairy Dust

Sparkling confetti

Magic Mirror

Watercolor paints   Ribbons
Paintbrush   Bows
Stickers

Magic Trunk

The contents of the Magic Trunk can be purchased, made, improvised, or imagined.

Magic Wand
Spell book
    (pocket-size notebook)
Crazy straws

Toy binoculars
Water soluble packing peanuts
Biodegradable (flushable)
    potty targets (see Resources)

Play Treats

Modeling clay
Bubbles
Stickers

Magic sponges
Washable markers

Grocery Store List

1 bottle carbonated water, mineral water, or clear soda
4–6 different fruit juices (apple, grape, cherry, orange, prune,
    mango, etc.)
1 quart milk, soymilk, or rice milk
Syrup or powder to make chocolate and strawberry milk
1 bottle of your child's favorite flavor soda
1 bottle each cola and prune juice if you want to make Pop Ups for a
    child who tends to be constipated
Miniature party cups that hold about 2 ounces
1 snack-size bag of M&Ms
1 small bag of fish-shaped crackers
1 small bag of pretzel thin mini-sticks
1 small bag of Hershey's Kisses in silver foil
½ cup peanut butter
1 stalk celery
½ cup apple sauce
Melon (in season)
1 small bag oyster crackers
2 cups powdered sugar
¼ cup milk (or soy or rice milk)
Red food coloring
Blue food coloring
Yellow food coloring
No-bake cookie mix

Presents and Prizes

Buy a small but significant present for your child from you and each family member, including Grandma and Granddad if they'll be coming to the Grand Finale Big Kid Celebration. Wrap these ahead of time.

Some Ideas

Magic cape

Foaming bath bubbles

Crystal (plastic) ball

Toys and games that encourage and reward your child for being curious and using his imagination

Silly string

Be sure to buy and wrap yourself a present as well. Get something that you really want!

Theme 2
Celebrity Star Salute

Get ready to walk down the Red Carpet because today you are one of the most rich and famous celebrities. Step up to the microphone, on to the stage, or in front of the camera and enjoy the applause! Don't be surprised if some of your biggest fans ask to have their picture taken with you, and watch out for those paparazzi cleverly disguised as Grandma and Granddad! Theme colors are red, black, silver, and gold.

DECORATIONS

Party Room: The Set (or the Stage)

In the Spotlight

Place a round white rug or slip-proof tablecloth on the floor as the Stage, or use ribbons and bows to rope off an area that can be used. If you have a floor lamp or track lights that can be directed toward the Stage, that adds a fun touch.

Fan Mail

Fill a bag with fan mail addressed to your child. Each letter should be a compliment. "You're great!" "You're the best!" "I love your talent!" "Stay sweet!" And the like. Make these ahead of time. The Fan Mail can be from people your child knows and also from celebrities or characters that he really likes. For example, "You can be a star, Love, Barney." Or "I hear you're going to be a big kid soon. Congratulations! SpongeBob."

Flowers from Admirers

Buy an assortment of whatever colorful flowers are in season (or use the silk variety) and place them around the room in vases with cards written to your child from various fans.

Star's Dressing Room: Bathroom Decorations

The Star's Dressing Room decorating ideas were generously contributed by Matt and Shari of *Room by Room* on HGTV. Check out their website at www.mattandshari.com.

Red Carpet

Paint a floor cloth (made out of natural canvas and coated with polyurethane) to look like a red carpet. It can be used in the hallway leading to the star's dressing room.

Star's Dressing Room

Using cardboard or poster board, create a star-shaped sign that is big enough for your child's name. Cover the sign with aluminum foil or paint it. Then paint your child's name on the star or write it using a thick magic marker.

Action!

Use poster board to create a movie clap board. "Lights. Camera. Action!" (You can also buy these at party and novelty stores.)

Encore

Hang several yards of red felt as an outside layer to the shower curtain. The felt could be parted in the middle and pulled to each side like a stage curtain would be.

Sparkle

Sprinkle some sparkling glitter on the bathroom counter.

Shine

Wrap star garland (found in card shops for wrapping presents) around the toilet paper holder, shower curtain rod, and your child's Potty Progress Chart.

Smile

Paint the outline of a large star on the bottom of the bathroom mirror—at the right height so that the star will frame your child's face when he looks into the mirror. Paint your child's name on the mirror above the star.

Center Stage

If you want to go all out, you can create (or hire someone to build) a wooden stage large enough to safely and comfortably accommodate your child and his potty-chair. To dress up the stage, paint old-time theater lights around the edges.

Celebrity Travel Trunk

The Celebrity Travel Trunk can be as small as a shoebox or as large as a suitcase. In fact, it can *be* a suitcase! The idea is to get a real suitcase or a cardboard box that you can paint and decorate.

The contents of the Celebrity Travel Trunk can be purchased, made, improvised, or imagined.

Microphone

Camera

Pen to sign autographs

Letter opener (child-safe) to open Fan Mail

Crazy straws

TREATS TRAY

Drinks

Sparkling Star Power

¼ cup carbonated water, mineral water, or clear soda

¾ cup fruit juice

Your child gets to add ¼ cup of carbonated water or clear soda, like Sprite, to fruit juice and say the magic words to make it fizz. Then your child can drink it while making a wish.

Movie Star Milk

Buy or mix flavored milks like chocolate and strawberry. If it's around the holidays, lots of kids love the taste of nonalcoholic eggnog. Dairy free varieties of milk and eggnog are also available in soy and rice.

Have your child pretend he's doing a commercial for milk and take his photo as he enjoys drinking it.

Celebrity Endorsement

1 or 2 ounces of soda measured out into a miniature cup.

Ask your child to pretend he's promoting the soda that he's drinking for a television or radio commercial. Take his photo and/or use the microphone to conduct an interview.

Bravo

2 ounces prune juice
1 ounce of cola

Mix well. Great for kids who tend to be constipated.
Your child bows to thank the audience, smiles, and then drinks.

Edible Treats

Famous Ms: one or two M&Ms
Say Cheese! one or two cubes of cheese (about the size of dice)
Applause: ¼ cup apple sauce
Sweet Success: one round slice banana, with a dab of peanut butter and a raisin on top
Celebrity Splurge: ½-inch thick slice of your child's favorite candy bar or cookie
Berry Rich: two sweet berries (blueberries, blackberries, or strawberries) with a sliver of chocolate
Carat Diamonds: two carrot slices, cut into diamond shapes
Popcorn: two pieces of popcorn or Cracker Jacks
If you don't want your child to eat treats made with refined sugar, check out the options available in health food stores.

Play Treats

All of these treats can be used during afternoon potty practice to help your child relax while sitting on the potty. Use the treats to keep your child engaged so he is willing to sit on the potty for several minutes at a time, too.

Star Keys: The key to the imaginary mansion or the keys to a brand-new pretend celebrity car.

Glitz and Glimmer: Shiny necklaces, bracelets, and earrings.

Special Effects: Mini container of bubbles with a bubble wand. The bubbles are a great activity for your child while he's sitting on his potty-chair.

Star Stickers: A few new stickers that your child can put on his Potty Progress Chart.

ACTIVITIES

Alternate between the activities listed below, the theme party books, and the potty-training books and videos.

Morning

Star-Shaped Jell-O

Make finger Jell-O in star-shaped molds or cut stars out of a tray of finger Jell-O using a star-shaped cookie cutter.

Photo Shoot

Take your child's photo and let him take Dolly's photo in a variety of different poses and with different backgrounds.

Awards Ceremony

Near the end of the morning, Dolly is awarded with a Star Pin for being a big kid. You tell your child that he can accept the award on Dolly's behalf and give her acceptance speech.

Afternoon

Potty Practice Activities

All of the following activities are designed to help make your child's experience of sitting on the potty-chair both fun and positive.

Signing Autographs

Your child can color or draw a picture and then sign it for his fans.

Creating Special Effects

Your child can blow bubbles while sitting in the Star Dressing Room.

Sit-Down Comedy

While your child is sitting on his potty-chair, have him entertain you with his comedy act, his singing, or by performing in whatever way he considers fun and playful.

Extra Interview!

Play the part of the celebrity interviewer and interview your child about his talent, his goals, and what it's like to be a star. (If you have a tape recorder you may want to record this interview and some of the other commercials or endorsements that your child does throughout the day.)

Theme Books

In addition to the potty-training books and videos listed in the Resources:

This Little Light of Mine (adapted by Raffi)
Has the stamp "Raffi Songs to Read" on the cover. Raffi Songs to Read
   are recognized as natural bridges between singing and reading.
Angelina and the Princess by Helen Craig and Katharine Holabird
This story is about a little mouse who hopes to perform for the ballet, but
   disaster strikes and she only wins a supporting role.
Willy the Dreamer by Anthony Browne (award winner)
Older children will love the evocative world of Willy and his day-
   dreams.

Bat Jamboree by Kathi Appelt
This story is about bats that come up with fabulous acts to entertain audiences.
The Remarkable Farkle McBride by John Lithgow
This book is about kids performing with instruments.

SHOPPING LISTS

Party Room Decorations

In the Spotlight
Round white rug or slip-proof tablecloth

Fan Mail
Stationery or cards and envelopes

Flowers from Admirers
Flowers (purchased ahead of time or delivered during the party)

Bathroom (Star's Dressing Room) Decorations

Red Carpet
Natural canvas floor cloth   Polyurethane
Red paint   Paintbrushes

Star Dressing Room and Clap Board
Cardboard or poster board   Paint
Aluminum foil   Paintbrush or thick Magic Marker

Encore
4–6 yards of red felt fabric

Sparkle
Sparkling glitter

Shine
Star garland

Smile

Paint	Large star shape to trace
Paintbrush	onto mirror

Center Stage

Wood boards	Paint
Carpentry tools	Paintbrush

Celebrity Travel Trunk

The contents of the Celebrity Travel Trunk can be imagined, purchased, made, or improvised.

Microphone	Letter opener (child-safe) to open
Camera	Fan Mail
Pen to sign autographs	Crazy straws

Play Treats

Toy keys or candy keys	Stickers
Toy jewelry	Crayons or washable markers
Bubbles	

Grocery Store List

1 bottle carbonated water, mineral water, or clear soda

4–6 different fruit juices (apple, grape, cherry, orange, prune, papaya, etc.)

1 quart milk, soymilk, or rice milk

Chocolate, strawberry, or other flavored milk

1 bottle of your child's favorite soda

1 bottle each cola and prune juice if you want to make Bravo for a child who tends to be constipated

Miniature party cups that hold about 2 ounces

Finger Jell-O mix

Star-shaped molds or casserole and cookie-cutters

1 snack-size bag of M&Ms

½ cup peanut butter

½ cup apple sauce

¼ cup each of two types of cheese

1 banana

⅓ cup raisins

1 candy bar or cookie (your child's favorite)

1 chocolate bar

½ cup of two or three types of berries

2 carrots

¼ cup popcorn or Cracker Jacks

Presents and Prizes

Buy a small but significant present for your child from you and each family member, including Grandma and Granddad, if they'll be coming to the Grand Finale Big Kid Celebration. Wrap these ahead of time.

Some Ideas

Candy ring

Candy necklace

Star-shaped pin

Trophy

Picture or poster of your child's favorite celebrity

Any item related to your child's interest or talent

Buy and wrap yourself a present too!

Theme 3

Seriously Silly Circus

Come one, come all, to the Greatest Show on Earth! The circus is in town and you get to play every part. Tame the tigers, ride the elephant, and tumble with the clowns. Walk the tightrope, dance with the bear, and prance with the poodles. Theme colors are bright red, blue, and yellow.

DECORATIONS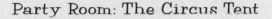

Party Room: The Circus Tent

The Center Ring

Paint a large circle (about 5–6 ft. diameter) on a large floor cloth or tarp. You can also make the Center Ring by taping a long piece of rope, ribbon, or yarn in a circle on the floor.

Silly Animals

To make the animals as silly as clowns, make them polka-dotted, plaid, and other fun patterns. The animals can be made out of fabric and stuffed. Or you can cut animal shapes out of foam core and glue on scraps of wallpaper or wrapping paper.

Decorating tip from Matt and Shari of *Room by Room* on HGTV

Friendly Audience

Set up a handful of chairs in a semicircle facing the Center Ring. Drape colorful bath towels (red, blue, and yellow) over the chairs. Fill the chairs with dolls, stuffed animals, or "pretend people." You can also tape photos of real people or your child's favorite cartoon characters to the chairs.

Balloon Drop

Buy a bag of the balloons that come in a variety of shapes. Fill them up, tie them to long ribbons, and hang them from the ceiling (using low-tack putty) over the heads of your Friendly Audience.

Back Stage: Bathroom Decorations

Back Stage Curtain

Make two panels of a back stage curtain by cutting an old sheet in half and decorating it with circus animals painted on with stencils, or cut out of felt or other fabric and glued or sewn to the sheet. (You can also begin with two panels of inexpensive curtains from a discount store.) Buy a spring tension rod that fits in your bathroom doorway. Slide the curtains onto the rod or attach the sheet panels by using extra large safety pins. Kids love going in and out of this curtain, which is very helpful during the afternoon portion of the potty party!

Silly Shower

Buy a large plastic circus-theme tablecloth at a party supply store and hang it on top of your regular shower curtain. Fill up brightly colored balloons and tie them to the shower curtain rings.

Decorating tip from Matt and Shari of *Room by Room* on HGTV

Clown Around

Paint or tape a clown hat on the bathroom mirror at a height that will make it fit on top of your child's head when he looks into the mirror. Paint your child's name on the mirror above or next to the hat.

Circus Trunk and Contents

Get a cardboard box that you can wrap, paint, and decorate as a circus trunk. The contents of the trunk can be purchased, made, improvised, or imagined.

Top hat   Sponge clown nose
Clown horns and noisemakers   Crazy straws
Tiger taming hoop   Silly string

TREATS TRAY

Drinks

Slow Slurp

¾ cup fruit juice

¼ cup carbonated water, mineral water, or clear soda

Your child can pretend that he is an elephant and the straw he is using is his trunk.

Monkey Milk

Buy or mix a cup or two of flavored milk like chocolate and strawberry. Dairy-free varieties of flavored milk are also available in soy and rice.

Have your child pretend he's a monkey before he drinks the milk.

Silly Sip

1 or 2 ounces of soda measured out into a miniature cup

Your child can pretend she's a clown. Let her make faces in a mirror before drinking her Silly Sip. She'll probably think this is more fun if you join in and make faces too.

Tiger Trick

2 ounces prune juice

1 ounce of cola

Mix well. Great for kids who tend to be constipated.

Your child sits up very tall—like a tiger sitting on its hind legs—and holds up her paws in front of her. You say, "Good tiger!" and give her the treat.

Edible Treats

Elephant Gems: two or three salted peanuts or other nuts that your child likes

Monkey 'Rounds: two or three round slices of banana

Cheesy Grin: one or two cubes of cheese (about the size of dice)

Circus Corn: two pieces of popcorn or Cracker Jacks

Tiger Tamers: one or two M&Ms

Clown Capers: one slice of your child's favorite candy bar or cookie (¼-inch to ½-inch thick)

Berry Fun: two sweet berries (blueberries, blackberries, or strawberries) with a tiny dab of whipped cream or yogurt

Circus Rings: two round carrot slices

If you don't want your child to eat treats made with refined sugar, check out the options available in health food stores.

Play Treats

All of these treats can be used during afternoon potty practice to help your child relax while sitting on the potty. Use the treats to keep her engaged so she is willing to sit on the potty for several minutes at a time, too.

Animal Sponges: Biodegradable (flushable) miniature sponges that expand to form animals when they are wet. (See Resources.)

Circus Stickers: A few new stickers that your child can put on her Potty Progress Chart.

Elephant Bubbles: Mini container of bubbles with a bubble wand. The bubbles are a great activity for your child while sitting on her potty-chair.

Clown Crayon: one extra-fat crayon

Paint Pen: one pen filled with nontoxic washable paint

ACTIVITIES

Alternate between the activities listed below, the theme party books, and the potty-training books and videos.

Morning

Tiger Taming

Take turns being the Tiger Tamer and the Tiger. Be sure to interact with Dolly, who is seated front and center in your friendly audience.

Elephant Rides

Your child can be the elephant and take Dolly for a ride around the house. If you can comfortably carry your child while crawling on your hands and knees, take a turn as the elephant and let your child ride on your back. (This can also be a great way to get your child to the bathroom in the afternoon.)

Swing, Dance, and Prance Like the Animals

Imitate the way circus animals move. Swing your arms like the monkeys and your long elephant trunk. Dance like the trick poodles, holding your paws up in front of you. Prance like the proud lions and let out a big roar.

(During the afternoon portion of the party, this is another way to get kids into the bathroom. "How would a monkey get to the bathroom?" "Let's have an elephant race to the potty!")

Upside-Down Clown

Help your child practice tumbling and rolling in the center ring, while making clown faces and laughing. Make a tightrope on the floor with a long piece of fat ribbon and let your child show off his balancing skills.

Lion Mask

Empty cereal box
Egg carton
1 sheet black paper

1 sheet white paper
3 plastic straws, cut in half
Paint: yellow, black, and orange or color markers

Use the front or back panel of an empty cereal box to make the mask. Cut out diamond shapes for eyes. Cut two ears out of the white paper and staple them onto the top of the box panel. Paint or color the box and the ears a yellowy-orange. Remove one pocket from the egg carton and paint or color it black. Attach it to the middle of the box for the lion's nose. Draw on the lion's mouth and freckles. Staple the straws for whiskers. Finally, cut the black paper into strips and curl. Attach to the top to form the lion's mane.

During the afternoon, encourage your child to wear the mask on the potty while he tells you a circus story, or while you tell or read him one.

Afternoon

Potty Practice Activities

All of the following activities are designed to help make your child's experience of sitting on the potty-chair both fun and effective.

Dancing Bear

To get your child into the bathroom, pretend you are a dancing bear and invite her to dance with you. Then, while leading the dance, maneuver her to the potty.

In Living Color

Your child can draw pictures or color in a circus theme coloring book.

Blowing Elephant Bubbles

While your child is sitting on the potty-chair, let her blow bubbles. She can pretend she is an elephant blowing the bubbles out of her trunk.

Clown Faces

Practice making happy, sad, angry, and just plain goofy faces with your child. Another variation of this activity is to draw the clown faces on white paper plates.

Silly Circus Sounds

This is a guessing game. Make the sound of an animal at the circus and let your child guess which animal sound you're making. Take turns with your child so that you both get to make sounds and guess the animals.

Circus Stories

Your child can wear his lion mask while he sits on the potty and tells you a circus story or while he listens to you tell him a story. Or, read one of the circus theme books together.

Theme Books

In addition to the potty-training books listed in the Resources:

Song of the Circus by Lois Duncan, illustrated by Meg Cundiff
Presenting the silliest romp ever seen under the big top!
If I Ran the Circus by Dr. Seuss
A grand circus story in grand Seussian style.
Olivia Saves the Circus by Ian Falconer
The story of the adorable little pig who remembers her trip to the circus very well. The performers were out sick, so she had to do everything herself.
The Man Who Walked Between the Towers by Mordicai Gerstein (Caldecott Medal Book)
The story of a young French aerialist, Philippe Petit, and his adventures walking, dancing, and performing tricks on a tightrope.
Mirette on the High Wire by Emily Arnold McCully (Caldecott Medal Book)
Sweeping watercolor paintings carry the reader over the rooftops of Paris and into the world of acrobats, jugglers, mimes, actors, and one resourceful little girl.
Circus Train by Joseph A. Smith
Story of a little boy who helps a circus train get to town after getting stuck on abandoned tracks in front of his house. Timothy has an idea that just might save the day.

Last Night I Dreamed a Circus by Maya Gottfried, paintings by Robert
    Rahway Zakanitch
In our dreams we can fly and juggle and twist and twirl.

SHOPPING LISTS

Party Room Decorations

Center Ring

Large floor cloth or
    waterproof tarp
Ribbons, paint, rope, or yarn
Polyurethane

Paintbrushes
Or simple outdoor picnic
    tablecloth

Silly Animals

Polka-dotted, plaid, and other
    zany fabric
And/or
Foam core
Wallpaper or wrapping paper

Pillow stuffing

Glue

Friendly Audience

4–5 chairs
Dolls or stuffed animals

Colorful bath towels

Balloon Drop

1 bag of variety-shaped
    balloons

Ribbon
Low-tack Putty

Bathroom (Back Stage) Decorations

Backroom Stage Curtain

Old sheet cut in half (or two inexpensive curtain panels)
Fabric paints
Paintbrushes
Stencils of animals

Glue, needle, and thread or sewing machine (for attaching circus animals to sheet)

Large safety pins

Spring tension rod that fits the width of the bathroom doorway

Silly Shower

1 large plastic circus theme tablecloth

Balloons (four or five in bright colors)

Clown Around Mirror

Watercolor paints

Paintbrush

Or picture of a clown hat

Circus Confetti

Brightly colored confetti for bathroom counter

Circus Trunk and Contents

Top hat

Clown horns and noisemakers

Tiger taming hoop

Sponge clown nose

Crazy straws

Decorative cups

Silly string

Play Treats

Biodegradable (flushable) potty targets (see Resources)

Circus stickers

Bubbles

1 extra-fat crayon

1 paint pen

Grocery Store List

1 bottle carbonated water, mineral water, or clear soda

4–6 different fruit juices (apple, grape, cherry, orange, prune, mango, etc.)

1 quart milk, soymilk, or rice milk

Syrup or powder to make chocolate and strawberry milk

1 bottle of your child's favorite soda

1 bottle *each* of cola and prune juice if you want to make Tiger Tricks for
     a child who tends to be constipated

Miniature party cups that hold about 2 ounces

Edible Treats

1 bag salted peanuts

2–3 bananas

Package of cubed cheese (or cut some the size of dice)

1 package popcorn or box of Cracker Jacks

1 snack-size bag of M&Ms

1 container fresh fruit (blueberries, blackberries, or strawberries)

1 can whipped cream, or 1 container yogurt

1–2 carrots

Activities

Lion Mask Supplies

Empty cereal box

Egg carton

1 sheet black paper

1 sheet white paper

3 plastic straws

Paints: yellow, black, and orange or
     color markers

Presents and Prizes

Buy a small but significant present for your child from you and each family
member, including Grandma and Granddad if they'll be coming to the
Grand Finale Big Kid Celebration. Wrap these ahead of time.

Some Ideas

Circus animal toys and/or masks

Face paints

Toys and games that stimulate creativity

Tickets to a real circus

Circus video tape or DVD

Buy and wrap a present for yourself, too, or assign this "support task" to your partner or a willing friend or
relative.

Theme 4

Teddy Bear Picnic

The Teddy Bears are having a picnic and everyone is invited! Spread out your Teddy Bear Blanket, decorate a Picnic Hat, and check out the surprises in your own special Picnic Basket. Don't wait too long to track the Paw Prints all the way to the Teddy Bear Tree House, where you can take a bubble-ball bath. Caution! The Teddy Bear Giggles often break out in the Tree House! Theme colors are outdoor colors like sky blue and grass green with splashes of your child's favorite colors.

DECORATIONS

Party Room: The Picnic Grounds

Picnic Blanket

Buy or paint a waterproof floor cloth or tarp in one of your child's favorite colors. Use this as the picnic blanket and the center of activity in the party room.

Cool Shade

Make tree trunks out of grocery bags that are cut open. Use green poster board for treetops. If you can make the trees taller than your child, that's even better! Nowadays, there are sticky tack materials that will allow you to hang things on the wall without harming the paint or wallpaper.

Picnic Tablecloth

Plastic red-and-white checkered tablecloths are easy to come by, and they clean up nicely too.

Ants!

If your child will think some plastic ants are fun, toss a few on the tablecloth and glue a few to your tree trunks.

Decorating tip from Matt and Shari of *Room by Room* on HGTV

Beary Good Friends

Invite all the teddy bears in the house to the picnic and consider inviting the other stuffed animals and dolls too. Be sure to give Dolly a reserved seat, right between you and your child.

Bear Cub Cooler

Get a cardboard box that has a lid. Paint and decorate it with teddy bear stickers or pictures of teddy bears cut out of magazines or from greeting cards. Fill with colorful paper plates and plastic or unbreakable dishes, cups, and utensils.

Bear Balloons

Order four bear-shaped helium balloons from a local balloon shop or florist and tie one to each corner of the Teddy Bear Blanket.

Teddy Bear Tree House: Bathroom Decorations

Tree House Door

Cover the outside of the bathroom door with white paper. With paint or fat markers, draw a big tree on the door. In the trunk of the tree, draw a door and write your child's name on it. You can also draw or cut out pictures of birds, squirrels, and other friendly forest animals that might visit the Teddy Bear Tree House, and place them in the tree.

Bubble-Ball Bath

Fill the bathtub with different size and color balls. Place one or more teddy bears in the bath.

Paw Prints

Make Bear Paw Prints out of construction paper and tape a trail of paw prints from the Picnic Ground to the Teddy Bear Tree House.

Picnic Basket and Contents

You can use a real picnic basket or make one out of a cardboard box. The contents of the basket can be purchased, made, improvised, and in some cases imagined.

Teddy bear coloring book
and crayons
Teddy bear tea set
Construction paper
Washable nontoxic markers

Glitter gel pen
Safety scissors
Teddy bear cookie cutter
Crazy straws

TREATS TRAY

Drinks

Fuzzy Wuzzy

¾ cup fruit juice
¼ cup carbonated water, mineral water, or clear soda

Before drinking, recite the old rhyme with your child: "Fuzzy Wuzzy was a bear, Fuzzy Wuzzy had no hair!"

Milk & Honey

1 cup milk (dairy, goat, rice, soy, or grain)
1 teaspoon honey

Milk and honey is a teddy bear's favorite drink. Drink it from a favorite cup or sip it with a crazy straw.

Pink Lemonade

1 ounce cranberry juice

1 cup lemonade

Serve from a small pitcher into plastic picnic cups.

Bubbly Bear

1 or 2 ounces of soda measured out into a miniature cup

Teddy Bear Punch

2 ounces prune juice

1 ounce of cola

Mix well. Great for kids who tend to be constipated. Serve in a party cup or plastic punch glass.

Edible Treats

Peanut Butter Bears: Peanut butter and jelly sandwiches cut into teddy bear shapes with a cookie cutter

Sticks and Stones: ½-inch celery stick with one nut or olive on top

Beary Bites: 2 sweet berries (blueberries, blackberries, or strawberries)

Teddy Bear Porridge: ¼ to ½ cup applesauce

Teddy Bear Buttons: 1 or 2 M&Ms

Melon Marbles: 1 or 2 melon balls

Gummy Bears: 1 or 2 gummy bear fruit candies

Cheese Paws: 1 round cracker with a slice of cheese

Play Treats

Most of these treats can be used during afternoon potty practice to help your child relax while sitting on the potty. Use the treats to keep him engaged so he is willing to sit on the potty for several minutes at a time, too.

Teddy Bear Sponges: Biodegradable (flushable) miniature sponges that expand to form teddy bears when they are wet. (See Resources.)

Teddy Bear and Picnic Stickers: A few new stickers that your child can put on his Potty Progress Chart.

Baby Bear Bubbles: Mini container of bubbles with a bubble wand. Bubbles are a great activity for your child while sitting on his potty-chair.

Teddy Bear Toothbrush

Paint Pen

ACTIVITIES

Alternate between the activities listed below, the theme party books, and the potty-training books and videos.

Morning

Teddy Bear Tales

Make up teddy bear stories and tell them to each other. Make sure you include Dolly.

Tea Time

Help your child serve make-believe tea or lemonade to all the dolls and bears at the picnic.

Picnic Hat

Your child can paint and decorate a store-bought straw hat. Buttons, beads, shells, and other small trinkets can be glued to the hat. Use bright ribbon to make a big bow.

Teddy Bear Face Paint

Using a face painting kit, paint your child's face like a teddy bear. If Dolly is washable, consider painting his face too.

Afternoon

Potty Practice Activities

All of the following activities are designed to help make your child's experience of sitting on the potty-chair both fun and positive.

Teddy Bear Giggles

This is a variation on the old camp game called Ha Ha! You say, "Ha!" Your child responds, "Ha, Ha." Then you say "Ha, Ha, Ha." The idea is to keep adding on one more "Ha" until you both burst into real laughter and giggles.

Baby Bear Bubbles

Encourage your child to blow bubbles while sitting on the potty-chair. You can try to pop them using one of the teddy bear's noses or your own nose.

Sunny Stories

Your child can wear the picnic hat he made while you take turns telling each other happy stories and recalling warm memories. (This is a great time to tell your child the story of the first word he said and his first steps. Be sure to express how proud you are with each new "first.")

Picnic Basket Bliss

Take turns naming things that you would love to pull out of a picnic basket. (It doesn't matter if these items would actually fit into a picnic basket.) "In my picnic basket, I have a diamond necklace!" "In my basket, I have a zillion chocolate cookies." "In my picnic basket, I have a pony!"

Theme Books

In addition to the potty-training books and videos listed in the Resources:

Corduroy by Don Freeman
Story of a little bear who has been on the department shelf for a long time and the little girl who wants to take him home.
The Teddy Bears' Picnic by Jimmy Kennedy
Adorable story of a picnic with all types of bears.
Floppy Teddy Bear by Patricia Lillie, pictures by Kathy Baker
Being a good big sister isn't always easy, especially when it comes to

patience and sharing. How can you share your very best thing if your sister is too little to take good care of it?

My Bear and Me by Barbara Maitland, pictures by Lisa Flather
A little girl and her teddy bear do everything together. Here they come ready for fun!

Where's My Teddy? by Jez Alborough
A little boy and his adventures over losing his favorite teddy bear.

SHOPPING LISTS

Party Room (Picnic Grounds) Decorations

Cool Shade

3–4 brown paper grocery bags
3 pieces of green poster board
Low-tack putty (or other sticky tack materials that won't harm paint or wallpaper)

Picnic Tablecloth

Plastic red-and-white-checked tablecloth

Plastic ants

Teddy Bear Blanket

Large floor cloth or tarp
Paint (in one of your child's favorite colors)

Polyurethane
Paintbrushes

Beary Good Friends

Teddy bears, stuffed animals, and dolls

Bear Cub Cooler

Cardboard box with lid
Teddy bear stickers
Pictures of teddy bears cut out of magazines or greeting cards
Colorful paper or plastic plates
Plastic and unbreakable dishes, cups, and utensils

Bear Balloons

4 helium bear-shaped balloons tied to ribbons

Bathroom (Teddy Bear Tree House) Decorations

Tree House Door

Roll of white butcher paper (or at least enough paper to cover the bathroom door)

Paint or fat markers

    Draw or cut out pictures of birds, squirrels, and other forest animals

Bubble-Ball Bath

Plastic balls in different sizes and colors

One or more stuffed teddy bears

Paw Prints

Paw prints made out of construction paper

Tape

Picnic Basket and Contents

Teddy bear coloring book and crayons	Safety scissors
	Glitter gel pen
Teddy bear tea set	Teddy bear cookie cutter
Construction paper	Crazy straws
Washable nontoxic markers	Decorated beverage cups

Grocery Store List

1 bottle carbonated water, mineral water, or clear soda

4–6 different fruit juices (apple, grape, cherry, orange, prune, mango, etc.)

1 quart of milk, soymilk, or rice milk

1 jar honey

1 bottle cranberry juice

1 bottle lemonade

1 bottle of your child's favorite soda

1 bottle *each* of cola and prune juice if you want to make Teddy Bear
Punch for a child who tends to be constipated

Miniature party cups that hold about 2 ounces

Edible Treats

Peanut butter, jelly, and bread

1 package celery

1 package nuts *or* small jar olives

1 container fresh fruit (blueberries, blackberries, or strawberries)

1 small jar applesauce

1 small package M&Ms

1 cantaloupe *or* honeydew melon

1 package gummy bear fruit candies

1 box crackers

1 package cheese

Play Treats

Biodegradable (flushable) potty targets (see Resources)

Teddy bear

Picnic theme stickers

Bubbles

New toothbrush

Children's paint pen

ACTIVITIES

Straw hat

Button, beads, yarn, and glue for hat

Nontoxic face painting kit

Presents and Prizes

Buy a small but significant present for your child from you and each family
member, including Grandma and Granddad if they'll be coming to the
Grand Finale Big Kid Celebration. Wrap these ahead of time.

Some Ideas

New teddy bear

Bear-shaped rug or blanket

Teddy bear outfit or accessory

Teddy bear photo frame

Teddy bear night light

Buy and wrap a present for yourself, too, or assign this support task to your partner or a willing friend or relative.

Theme 5

Super Hero Saves the Day

Hip Hip Hooray! You saved the day! Team up with your favorite cartoon character or join forces with real-life heroes like firefighters and police officers. Climbing, jumping, running, and flying are part of a super hero's everyday life. Catch a bad guy, put out a fire, rescue a kitten, and maybe even turn back time! Theme colors are bright, bold colors like fire-truck red and cobalt blue highlighted with metallic colors like silver and gold.

DECORATIONS

Party Room: The Rescue Room

Action Arena

Use colorful ribbons and streamers to mark the boundaries of a safe play space where all super hero action will take place. Place exercise mats (or several layers of thick blankets) on the floor to facilitate and soften tumbling activities.

Super Hero Command Station

Protect an upholstered sofa with a waterproof tarp or blanket and then cover it with a bright bedspread, blanket, or sheet.

Super Hero Banner

Cut an old twin-size bed sheet in half, lengthwise. Paint your child's name on the banner in giantsize letters and hang the banner on the wall.

Super Hero Recharging Room: Bathroom Decorations

Recharging Room Door

Cover the bathroom door with white or bright color paper and paint a large control panel with different color buttons at your child's eye level. Paint super hero symbols on the door and glue or tape super hero pictures and recent photos of your child on the door.

Power Board

Use a 10-inch square of foam core or poster board to make a Super Hero Recharging Panel. Paint the board or cover it with construction paper. Cut out two red circles, each about 3 inches in diameter, and glue or tape them side by side on the recharging panel.

(In the morning, when Dolly sits on the potty-chair, your child can place her hands on the recharging circles. In the afternoon, when your child sits on the potty-chair, she can also place her hands on the recharging circles. The longer she sits there "recharging," the more power she has when she's done.)

Power Panel

Tape a large blue square of poster board on the ceiling above the potty-chair. Hang a dozen 3- or 4-foot-long colorful streamers from the square.

Super Hero Locker and Contents

Get a large cardboard box that you can wrap, paint, or decorate as a Super Hero Locker. The contents of the Super Hero Locker can be purchased, made, improvised, and imagined.

Super Hero Cape or Uniform

Helmet
Belt
Special equipment (e.g., radio, flashlight, handcuffs)
Binoculars

TREATS TRAY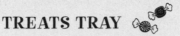

Drinks

Power Potion

¾ cup fruit juice

¼ cup carbonated water, mineral water, or clear soda

Show your child how to make a muscle by making a fist and bending his elbow. Say something like, "Wow! you're strong!"

Jumping Juice

1 or 2 ounces soda measured out into a miniature cup

After jumping up and down five times, your child gets to drink the Jumping Juice.

Flying Fuel

Buy or mix a cup or two of flavored milks like chocolate and strawberry. If it's around the holidays, lots of kids love the taste of nonalcoholic eggnog. Dairy-free varieties of milk and eggnog are also available in soy and rice.

Turbo Charge

2 ounces prune juice

1 ounce of cola

Mix well. Great for kids who tend to be constipated.

Turbo Charge is the perfect fuel for a race to the potty. Your child drinks the juice and then races you to the Super Hero Recharging Room.

Edible Treats

Victory Vitamins: one or two berries or cherries

Power Tower: 1-inch celery stick with peanut (or other nut) butter

Speed Stick: 1-inch-long thinly sliced carrot stick

Strong Sauce: ¼ cup applesauce

American Pride: two dice-size cubes of American cheese
Super Sweet: one M&M
Rescue Rope: one pretzel
Power Surge: ½-inch-slice of your child's favorite candy bar or cookie
> If you don't want your child to eat treats made with refined sugar, check out the options available in health food stores.

Play Treats

Most of these treats can be used during afternoon potty practice to help your child relax while sitting on the potty. Use the treats to keep your child engaged so she is willing to sit on the potty for several minutes at a time, too.

Magic Sponges

Biodegradable (flushable) miniature sponges that expand into shapes when they're wet. (See Resources.)
Crazy straws
Super hero stickers
Service badges (police, firefighter, super hero)

ACTIVITIES

Alternate between the activities listed below, the theme party books, and the potty-training books and videos.

Morning

Heroic Rescue

Oh no! Dolly has climbed the tree to rescue the kitten, and now they're both stuck up there! Super Hero to the rescue! This is just one example of a rescue scene that you and your child can enact together.

Super Hero Training

Jumping, hopping, skipping, standing on one foot, rolling, tumbling, and pretend flying are part of a super hero's daily fitness routine. Keep the training session within the safe boundaries of the Action Arena.

Fire Fighting

A fire has erupted in the Action Arena and fortunately your Super Hero is ready and able to put it out. You can pretend the fire is there or you can spray some Silly String and call it a fire.

Afternoon

Potty Practice Activities

The following activities are designed to help make your child's experience of sitting on the potty-chair both fun and positive.

Recharging

Your super hero can recharge his power by sitting on the potty-chair and placing her hands on top of the red circles on her Power Board.

Super Hero Stories

Read a book to your super hero while she's sitting on her potty-chair, or let her look at the pictures and tell you the story.

Super Hero Salute

Take turns naming real-life and fictional super heroes who deserve praise. Clap your hands and cheer after each name (or role) is mentioned.

Super Hero Interview

While your super hero is sitting on her potty-chair, interview her about her latest super hero adventure. Ask her what happened, who was involved, and what she did to save the day.

Theme Books

In addition to the potty-training books listed in the Resources:

Froggy Goes to the Doctor by Jonathan London, illustrated by Frank Remkiewicz

Cute story about a little frog who doesn't want to go for his check-up. But with Froggy for a patient, it's the doctor who should be nervous!

Curious George Goes to the Hospital by H. A. Rey and Margret Rey

It all begins when George swallows a piece of a jigsaw puzzle and has to go to the hospital. In the end everything comes out all right, including the piece of puzzle that started it all.

Clifford the Firehouse Dog by Norman Bridwell

Adventures about the day Clifford went to visit his brother, a fire rescue dog who lives at the firehouse. Includes a list of fire safety rules parents can share with their children.

Policeman Small by Lois Lenski

A tale about Policeman Small and his daily duties in Tinytown.

At the Firehouse by Anne Rockwell

A friendly Dalmatian dog loves fire engines. He wants to know everything about being a fireman, and one day he gets his chance to sit in the big fire truck and feel like a real firefighter.

SHOPPING LISTS

Party Room (Rescue Room) Decorations

Action Area

Colorful ribbons and streamers
Exercise mats *or* several layers of thick blankets

Super Hero Command Station

Waterproof tarp *or* blanket
Bright colorful bedspread, blanket, or sheet

Super Hero Banner

Old bed sheet
Paint
Paintbrushes
Tacks *or* low-tack putty (to hang banner)

Bathroom (Super Hero Recharging Room) Decorations

Recharging Room Door

Roll of white butcher paper or brightly colored paper (enough to cover bathroom door)

Glue or tape

Pictures of your child's favorite super hero

Recent photos of your child

Paint

Paintbrush (to make large control panel on paper)

Power Board

10-inch square of stiff cardboard or poster board to make recharging panel

Paint or cover with red construction paper

Glue or tape

Power Panel

Tape or low-tack putty

Large blue square of poster board

Colorful streamers

Super Hero Locker and Contents

Large cardboard box

Super hero wrapping paper

Super Hero Cape or Uniform

Helmet

Belt

Toy binoculars

Special equipment (e.g., radio, flashlight, handcuffs)

Grocery Store List

1 bottle carbonated water, mineral water, or clear soda

4–6 different fruit juices (apple, grape, cherry, orange, prune, mango, etc.)

1 quart milk, soymilk, or rice milk

Syrup or powder to make chocolate and stawberry milk

1 bottle of your child's favorite soda

1 bottle each cola and prune juice if you want to make a Turbo Charge drink for a child who tends to be constipated

Miniature party cups that hold about 2 ounces

Edible Treats

1 container fresh fruit (blueberries, blackberries, cherries, or strawberries)

Package of celery sticks

Jar of peanut (or other nut) butter

1–2 carrots

Small jar of applesauce

Package of cubed cheese (or cut some the size of dice)

1 snack-size bag of M&Ms

Child's favorite candy bar or cookies

Play Treats

Biodegradable (flushable) potty targets (see Resources)

Crazy straws

Decorative beverage cups

Super hero stickers

Service badges (police, firefighter, super hero)

Presents and Prizes

Buy a small but significant present for your child from you and each family member, including Grandma and Granddad if they'll be coming to the Grand Finale Big Kid Celebration. Wrap these ahead of time.

Some Ideas

Super hero (or real-life hero) uniform

Super hero big kid underpants

Super hero book or movie

Trophy

Picture or poster of your child's favorite super hero

The Super Hero's Mom also gets a present. Buy yourself something special.

Theme 6

Splish Splash Beach Bash

The sky is blue and the sun is shining, so grab your beach bag and head for the shore! Swim with the dolphins, ride on a sea turtle, and surf the big waves! Ready for more fun and games? Race to the Boardwalk where you can fish for prizes, play beach basketball, get a tattoo, and have your toenails painted! Theme colors are powder blue, deep turquoise, and sunny yellow.

DECORATIONS

Party Room: The Beach

Beach Blanket

Lay a waterproof tarp or blanket on the floor and cover it with a large beach blanket, old bedspread, or several large colorful beach or bath towels.

Beach Bucket

A small plastic bucket with a handle that will be easy for your child to carry.

High Tide

Use a long cardboard box or a few pieces of thick poster board to make the water's edge. Cut the cardboard so it's about six inches high and a few feet long (or you can tape or staple pieces together to make it three or four feet wide). Paint the cardboard water blue. Tape it between two beach chairs and make sure there's some open space out in the water for your child to swim and play in.

Ocean Life

Place some toy fish out in the Ocean (plastic, stuffed, or inflatable). Cut two or three seagulls out of white poster board and hang them from the ceiling. (Don't worry about precise reproductions! Kids at this age are great at pretending, so simply declaring that the big white Vs hanging from the ceiling are "birds" will work.)

Bathroom Boardwalk: Decorations

Boardwalk Entry

Cover the bathroom door with white paper and paint or draw a large archway on the paper. Draw or glue pictures of things that might be on an ocean boardwalk like a Ferris wheel, saltwater taffy, or cotton candy.

Beach Basketball Hoop

Tie ribbons to a laundry basket or decorate a cardboard box to serve as the basket.

Fish Pond

Buy a dozen colorful Ping-Pong balls and use a Sharpie to number the balls from 1 through 12. Put the balls in the bathtub. Put a large plastic spoon next to the fish pond.

Sun Showers

Paint an inexpensive clear shower curtain with a bright yellow sun above crystal blue water.

Decorating tip from Matt and Shari of *Room by Room* on HGTV

Beach Bag and Contents

You can use a real beach bag or decorate a large pillowcase. The contents of the Beach Bag can be purchased, made, improvised, or imagined.

Inflatable water float   Water bottle
Inflatable beach ball   Crazy straws
Binoculars

TREATS TRAY

Drinks

Sunny Sip

1 cup lemonade

Serve in a clear plastic cup. Before your child drinks it, help her to hold it up in front of a light and make it shine like the sun.

Beach Blast

¾ cup fruit juice
¼ cup carbonated water, mineral water, or clear soda

Serve in a plastic cup that your child decorates with stickers.

Wave

1 cup dairy, soy, or rice milk
Optional: 1 tablespoon chocolate or strawberry flavoring

Pour liquid into a clear *plastic* jar. Close lid tightly. Help your child to hold the plastic jar with both hands. Gently rock it back and forth to make waves.

Sea Foam

2 ounces prune juice
1 ounce cola

Great for kids who tend to be constipated.

Edible Treats

Beach Balls: one or two melon balls
Crazy Crunch: two circular carrot slices

Tooty Fruity: one *pitted* cherry (cut in half) and one seedless grape (cut in half)

Hot Dog Rings: two thin round slices of a cooked hotdog (beef, turkey, or soy) with a drop or two of ketchup

Fish & Chips: two fish-shaped crackers or fish-shaped pretzels and two potato or corn chips

Cotton Candy: a cotton ball–size serving in a miniature paper cup

Fruit Ice: ¼ cup fruit ice, frozen yogurt, or sorbet

Saltwater Taffy: one thin sliver of soft taffy

Play Treats

Most of these treats can be used during afternoon potty practice to help your child relax while sitting on the potty. Use the treats to keep your child engaged so he is willing to sit on the potty for several minutes at a time, too.

Beach, Ocean, or Fish Stickers

Beach Bubbles: Mini container of bubbles with a bubble wand. The bubbles are a great activity for your child while sitting on his potty-chair.

Magic Sponges: Biodegradable (flushable) miniature sponges that expand into shapes when wet.

Crazy Straws

Sandcastle Clay: Mini container of modeling clay.

ACTIVITIES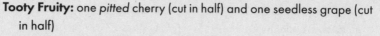

Alternate between the activities listed below, the theme party books, and the potty-training books and videos.

Morning

Beach Hat

Cut a large circle (about 12-inch diameter) out of stiff white cardboard. In the center of that circle, draw a small circle (about 2.5-inch diameter). Cut the small circle out so that the "rim" of the hat will fit on your child's head. Use washable markers, paints, and stickers to decorate the hat. Your child can also glue objects like seashells, beads, and pipe cleaners to the hat.

Seashell Hunt

Hide seashells around the party room and on the Boardwalk. Your child can use his beach bucket to collect the shells as he finds them.

Surf's Up

Pretend you and your child are playing in the water. Swim with the dolphins, ride on a sea turtle, and surf the big waves.

Make Waves

Large clear *plastic* soda bottle   Blue food coloring

Vegetable oil   Water

Rinse bottle and remove labels. Fill half of the plastic bottle with water. Add about 1 tablespoon of oil. Add a few drops of blue food coloring. Tightly screw on the bottle cap. Your child can gently rock the bottle back and forth to create waves.

Afternoon

Potty Practice Activities

The following activities are designed to help make your child's experience of sitting on the potty-chair more enjoyable and successful.

Go Fish

Every time Dolly and your child use the potty, they get to fish for a ball. The large plastic spoon is the fishing pole. (If it's too difficult for your child to fish with the spoon, let him fish with one hand. The idea is for him to enjoy himself, not to become frustrated or disappointed.) Each ball corresponds to a category of prizes. 1–4 = sticker for Potty Chart; 5–8 = trinket to tape on Boardwalk Entry; 9–12 = your child's choice from the treat tray.

Beach Basketball

Place a basket close enough to the potty-chair to ensure your child can toss the ball in. As his skill and confidence grows, pull the basket back very gradually, staying well within victory range.

Tootsy Toes

Little girls love to have their toenails and fingernails painted and lots of little boys think it's fun too. While your child is sitting on the potty, paint his toenails and/or fingernails. You can paint just one or two each time. You can paint them different colors or all the same. (You can remove the polish at the end of the day, so unless you're expecting a visit from the fashion police, don't worry about how the manicure or pedicure looks. The idea is for your child to enjoy sitting on the potty-chair—not to make a fashion statement.)

Tattoo Time

Find some cool beach or ocean theme temporary tattoos. Pretend you are a tattoo artist and your child is the customer.

I Spy

Take turns spying things that might be on the beach, the boardwalk, or in the ocean.

Beach Bubbles

Your child can pretend he's a fish blowing bubbles.

Theme Books

In addition to the potty-training books listed in the Resources:

At the Beach by Anne and Harlow Rockwell
There's so much to do at the beach! There are sand castles to build, seashells to gather, and a picnic lunch to enjoy in the shade of a bright beach umbrella.
Just Grandma and Me by Mercer Mayer
Funny misadventures during a day at the beach.

Beach Babble by Kimberley Knutson
Celebrate the spirit of the seashore in this almost audible depiction of a sparkling summer day at the beach.
On the Way to the Beach by Henry Cole
Find a place to sit and watch and listen to all the sights and sounds on the way to the beach.
Beach Day by Karen Roosa, illustrated by Maggie Smith
Waves lapping, sails snapping, chicken eggs, and deviled eggs . . . One family's perfect day is captured in buoyant verse and playful illustrations.

SHOPPING LISTS

Party Room Decorations

Beach Blanket

Waterproof tarp or blanket
Large beach blanket, old bedspread, or several large beach and bath towels

Beach Bucket

Small plastic bucket with handle

High Tide

Long cardboard box or a few pieces of thick blue poster board
Paint
Paintbrushes
Tape

Ocean Life

Plastic, stuffed, or inflatable toy fish
White poster board
Pictures of birds

Bathroom (Boardwalk) Decorations

Boardwalk Entry

Roll of white butcher paper or enough white paper to cover the bathroom door

Paint, markers, or glue

Pictures of things you might see at the boardwalk: Ferris wheel, saltwater taffy, and cotton candy

Beach Basketball Hoop

Cardboard box or laundry basket

Ribbons or streamers

Sun Showers

Clear shower curtain

Yellow paint

Blue paint

Paintbrushes

Beach Bag and Contents

Use a real beach bag or decorate a large pillowcase

Inflatable water float

Inflatable beach ball

Binoculars

Water bottle

Crazy straws

Decorative cups

Grocery Store List

Lemons, sugar, and water (for fresh-squeezed lemonade)

1 bottle carbonated water, mineral water, or clear soda

4–6 different fruit juices (apple, grape, cherry, orange, prune, mango, etc.)

1 quart milk, soymilk, or rice milk

Syrup or powder to make chocolate and strawberry milk

1 bottle of your child's favorite soda

1 bottle each cola and prune juice if you want to make Sea Foam for a child who tends to be constipated

Miniature party cups that hold about 2 ounces

Cantaloupe or honeydew melon

1–2 carrots

Package of *pitted* cherries or seedless grapes

Hotdogs (beef, turkey, or soy)

Package of fish-shaped crackers *or* fish-shaped pretzels

Small package of baked potato or corn chips

Package of cotton candy

Frozen-fruit ice cups or sticks, frozen yogurt, or sorbet

Saltwater taffy

Play Treats

Beach, ocean, or fish stickers

Bubbles

Crazy straws

Decorative cups

Mini container of modeling clay

Biodegradable (flushable) potty targets (see Resources)

Activities List

White stiff cardboard

Scissors

Washable markers or paints

Stickers

Glue

Seashells, feathers, and pipe cleaners

Presents and Prizes

Buy a small but significant present for your child from you and each family member, including Grandma and Granddad if they'll be coming to the Grand Finale Big Kid Celebration. Wrap these ahead of time.

Some Ideas:

Beach towel

Bathing suit *or* trunks

A visit to the local pool or water park

Sandals or flip-flops

Beach chair

Face mask or eye goggles

Buy and wrap a present for yourself, too, or ask your partner or a willing friend or relative to buy and wrap it for you. Make sure you tell them exactly what you want!

Theme 7

Fun on the Farm

Pony rides and tractor pulls, sunflowers to sow, and fields to mow—let's have fun on the farm! Use your little Red Wagon to deliver horse feed to the barn, carry your spade and watering can to the garden patch, and give your furry friends free rides. Make a farm animal collage and play Leap, Hop, and Slither! Theme colors are muted reds, vibrant greens, and soft blues.

DECORATIONS

Party Room: The Farm

Barnyard

Spread a large waterproof tarp on the floor and cover it with a green blanket or sheet. Or paint a floor cloth grass green and coat it with polyurethane. Place large plastic flowerpots, filled with bright silk or plastic flowers, at each of the four corners of the Barnyard.

Tractor

Get a cardboard box that's large enough for your child to sit in. Cut the top off the box. Cut an opening on one side of the box so that your child can step into the box. Place a small bench, stool, or pillow inside the box as the tractor seat. Paint a steering wheel on the inside front of the box. Paint the outside of the box green, or cover it with green poster board or construction paper. Cut two large wheels (about 12-inch diameter) out of black construction paper and tape them onto the back of the tractor. Cut two small wheels (about 5-inch diameter) out of black construction paper and tape them onto the front of the tractor.

Giant Sunflowers

Buy a handful of sunflower helium-filled balloons and arrange them around the party room. You can also use bright yellow balloons or make sunflowers out of construction paper. Use low-tack putty to hang them on the walls.

Barn: Bathroom Decorations

Barn Door and Hayloft

Cover the outside of the bathroom door with red paper. Using white paint or construction paper, make the outline of a barn door. Above the barn door outline, make a large white rectangle for the hayloft. Cut bales of hay out of yellow construction paper and glue or tape them into the hayloft.

Pony Stall

Cover the bottom of the bathtub with a thin layer of straw, shredded yellow paper, or beige Easter basket grass. Set a red feed bucket filled with granola in the stall. Tape brown paper or poster board to the back wall above the tub. Using a black marker, draw horizontal lines on the paper about one foot apart to make the wall look like it is made of wood boards. If you happen to have a toy rocking horse, spring horse, or stick horse, put it in the stall. Otherwise, you and your child can imagine the pony.

Farm Animal Scene

Cut pictures of farm animals (horses, cows, pigs, chickens, roosters, dogs and puppies, cats and kittens) out of a coloring book and glue them to a large sheet of green poster board. Hang the poster board on the inside of the bathroom door.

Little Red Wagon and Contents

If your child already has a wagon, decorate it for the party by taping some ribbons to it and putting farm stickers on it. If your child doesn't have a wagon, you can buy one or improvise. (To improvise, paint a wagon-size box red, both inside and out. Attach a rope to the bottom of the box so your child can pull it around.)

The contents of the wagon can be purchased, made, imagined, or improvised.

Farm Friends: Stuffed toy kitten, puppy, or both
Horse Feed: Plastic container with lid, filled with 1 cup of granola
Crayons
Gardening Tools: Toy rake and spade
Carrots: 1 small bunch of fresh carrots with green carrot tops
Small Flower Pot
Small Watering Can
Topsoil: 4–6 cups in a sealed plastic bag
Sunflower Seeds: one package

TREATS TRAY

Drinks

Farm Fresh Milk

1 cup warm milk (cow, goat, soy, or rice)

Fruit Spritzer

¾ cup fruit juice (apple, cherry, or grape)
¼ cup carbonated water, mineral water, or clear soda

Invite your child to help you pick the imaginary fruit and pretend to squeeze it into the cup. Then pour in the juice.

Silo Sip

1 or 2 ounces of soda in a miniature cup
Serve in a tall, thin plastic cup or plastic popsicle mold

Cockadoodledoo

2 ounces prune juice
1 ounce of cola

Mix well. Great for kids who tend to be constipated.

Show your child how to crow like a rooster before drinking the Cock-adoodledoo. Flap your wings like a rooster by tucking your hands into your armpits and raising and lowering your elbows; encourage your child to imitate you.

Edible Treats

Bunny Bites: 2 bite-size pieces of carrot

Tractor Wheel: 1 round cracker with a piece of cheese

Apple Tart: Apple slice with 1 teaspoon yogurt on top

Wild Blackberries: 1 or 2 blackberries

Animal Crackers: 1 or 2 animal-shaped crackers

Fudge Ribbon: 1 very thin slice of fudge, about the size and shape of a toothpick

Fence Posts: 2 1-inch pretzel sticks

Barn Door: 1 graham cracker

Play Treats

Most of these treats can be used during afternoon potty practice to help your child relax while sitting on the potty. Use the treats to keep your child engaged so she is willing to sit on the potty for several minutes at a time, too.

Markers (washable, nontoxic)

Crazy Straws

Farm Stickers

Animal Sponges: Biodegradable (flushable) miniature sponges that expand to form animals when they are wet. (See Resources.)

ACTIVITIES

Alternate between the activities listed below, the theme party books, and the potty-training books and videos.

Morning

Sunflower Sowing

Help your child fill the flowerpot with soil. Give her three seeds to press into the soil. Help her water the seeds and set the planter on a sunny windowsill.

Pony Rides

Each time Dolly uses the potty, she gets to have a pony ride on your child's back or on yours.

Animal Collage

Calendar or several magazines with photos of farm animals
Poster board
Safety scissors
Glue or paste

    Help your child cut out pictures of animals. Encourage her to arrange them however she likes on the poster board. (Resist the urge to make suggestions.) Help your child to glue or paste the pictures onto the poster board. When the glue is dry, hang it on the wall at your child's eye level. Help your child learn the names of the animals and the sounds they make.

Afternoon

Potty Practice Activities

Most of the following activities are designed to help make your child's experience of sitting on the potty-chair both fun and positive.

Leap, Hop, and Slither

This is a great way to get your child to the bathroom. Name an animal and then race to the bathroom moving the way that animal would move. If you say, "Frog!" you both leap and hop. If you say "Snake," you slither.

Old MacDonald Had a Farm

This song can go on for as long as you like (or as long as you can stand it). Once you run out of farm animals, you can put in farm objects like shovels, rakes, and tractors and have fun making their sounds.

Pony Rides

When your child uses the potty, she gets to have a pony ride on your back or she gets to give her doll a pony ride.

Farm Friends Coloring

Each time your child uses the potty, she gets to color one of the farm animals on the back of the barn door.

Wagon Wishes

This is a creativity and imagination game. Say, "I wish I had a wagon that could . . ." and then fill in the blank. Take turns with your child. There are no wrong answers and the wish doesn't have to actually be able to fit in a wagon. The sillier and more outrageous the wishes are, the more your child is likely to enjoy this game. For example, I wish I had a wagon that could make chocolate chip cookies; turn into a pony; fly!

Theme Books

In addition to the potty-training books listed in the Resources:

Barnyard Banter by Denise Fleming
It's another noisy morning on the farm with lots of farm animals.
Barn Sneeze by Karen B. Winnick
One night the wind blows through the barn and causes Cow to sneeze, which sets off a sneezy chain reaction.
Big Red Barn by Margaret Wise Brown, pictures by Felicia Bond
By the author of *Goodnight Moon*. Simple story about the cycle of a day on the farm, where a family of animals peacefully plays and sleeps.

Color Farm by Lois Ehlert
Simple story of animals, shapes, and colors.
Spots, Feathers, and Curly Tails by Nancy Tafuri
What has spots? A cow has spots. The author knows what questions her
    young fans will love to hear—and answer!

SHOPPING LISTS

Party Room Decorations

Barnyard

Large waterproof tarp
Green blanket or sheet

Large plastic flowerpots
Bright silk or plastic flowers

Tractor

Large cardboard box
    (large enough for
    child to sit in)
Small bench, stool, or pillow

Paint (green and black)
Paintbrush
Or construction paper
Tape

Giant Sunflowers

6–12 sunflowers or bright yellow helium balloons attached to long
    strings
Construction paper sunflowers
Tape or string

Bathroom (Barn) Decorations

Barn Door and Hayloft

Enough red construction paper to cover entire bathroom door
Enough white construction paper to make outline of barn door
2–3 pieces of yellow construction paper
Glue or painter's tape

Pony Stall

Straw, shredded yellow paper, or beige Easter basket grass
Red pail or bucket
Brown paper or poster board
Thick black marker
Toy rocking horse, spring horse, or stick horse
1 cup granola

Farm Animal Scene

Pictures of farm animals   Large sheet of green construction
Glue   paper

Little Red Wagon and Contents

Red wagon or box painted red with rope attached
Ribbons and bows
Farm stickers

The Wagon's contents can be purchased, made, improvised, or imagined.

Stuffed toy kitten, puppy, or both   Small flowering pot
Plastic container with lid   Small watering can
Crayons   4–6 cups topsoil in a sealed
Toy rake and spade   plastic bag
1 small bunch fresh carrots   1 package sunflower seeds
    with green carrot tops

Grocery Store List

1 bottle carbonated water, mineral water, or clear soda
4–6 different fruit juices (apple, grape, cherry, orange, prune,
    mango, etc.)
1 quart milk, soymilk, or rice milk
1 bottle of your child's favorite soda
1 bottle each of cola and prune juice if you want to make Cockadoodle-
    doos for a child who tends to be constipated
Miniature party cups that hold about 2 ounces

Edible Treats

Small bag prepared carrots
Package of crackers
Your child's favorite cheese
1–2 apples
Yogurt

Package of blackberries
Package of animal-shaped crackers
Small package of fudge
Miniature pretzel sticks
Graham crackers

Play Treats

Markers (washable and nontoxic)
Crazy straws
Biodegradable (flushable) potty targets (see Resources)
Farm stickers

Activity Supply List

Calendar or several magazines with photos of farm animals
Poster board
Safety scissors
Glue or paste

Presents and Prizes

Buy a small but significant present for your child from you and each family member, including Grandma and Granddad if they'll be coming to the Grand Finale Big Kid Celebration. Wrap these ahead of time.

Some Ideas

* Farm visit
Toy farm
Toy farm animals
Toy tractor

Toddler-Size Garden: A small square of yard or a window box that you give to your child and you plant and care for together.

Farm Visit: Depending on the time of year, you and your child can make plans to visit a farm. For example, around Halloween and

Thanksgiving there are pumpkin farms. Before Christmas, there are Christmas tree farms. At other times of the year there are vegetable farms, orchards, dairy farms, flower farms, and sheep and goat farms. Make arrangements ahead of time.

Buy and wrap a present for yourself, too, or assign this support task to your partner or a willing friend or relative.

Theme 8

The Princess Ball

Dance at the Princess Ball and dine at the formal banquet table. Recline in the Princess Lounge Chair, ride in the Royal Carriage, and relax on your very own throne. Make your own Princess Necklace and decorate your Carriage Mask. Use crayons, markers, and your very own wishes to color in the details of your royal life. Theme colors are pale pinks, soft whites, and metallic silver.

DECORATIONS

Party Room: The Castle

Ballroom Floor

To make the outline of a ballroom floor, tape a long silver ribbon to the floor in a circle, square, or rectangle. Make sure it is large enough for you and your child to dance in together.

Princess's Lounge Chair

Cover the sofa with a waterproof blanket or rug. On top of that place a pink bedspread or sheet. Attach a large silver bow to each end of the sofa.

Banquet Table for Three

Beautifully set a table, complete with fresh flowers, linen, china, and crystal. Set a place for you, your princess, and Dolly. (Don't stress out. You can designate the banquet table as a place for pretend food.)

Royal Carriage: Bathroom Decorations

Carriage Door

Cover the bathroom door with white paper. Draw the side door of a carriage on the bathroom door. (Draw the bottom of the door low enough that your child could step in if it were real.) Paint or color the area above the carriage door light blue (for the sky). Paint or color the area beneath the door light pink (the color of royal roads).

Princess Vanity

Use a child's toy vanity or lay a pretty pink towel on the bathroom counter. Place hair bows, brushes, fingernail polish, makeup, and anything else the Princess might need to get ready for the ball.

Princess Throne

Use sequins, glitter, or small shiny beads spray-mounted or hot-glued to the Throne in places that won't touch bare skin. Set princess throne inside canopy.

Lay a purple and gold floor cloth as a rug leading up to the throne.

Decorating tip from Matt and Shari of *Room by Room* on HGTV

Princess Canopy

I suggest purchasing the Disney Princess Canopy, a sheer drift of white nylon tulle that flows from a Princess Crown with a felt pom-pom trim. The canopy is 118 inches long, and it includes ties for hanging it from a ceiling hook. This is a gorgeous way to entice your child to sit on the potty. After the party, you can move the canopy to your child's bedroom. (You can also make your own Princess Canopy.)

To make a canopy, go to a craft store and buy a hoop that is 18 to 24 inches in diameter. The hoop can be made of wood, metal, or sturdy plastic. Buy a piece of white, pink, or lavender netting that is about 10 feet long and 4–5 feet wide. Tie three 12-inch white ribbons to the hoop. Then tie the ribbons together at the top. Attach the short side of the netting to the hoop with double-stick tape or hot glue from a glue gun. Hang the canopy from a ceiling hook by the ribbons.

Castle Grounds

Fill the bathtub with pillows covered with green pillowcases. Tape powder blue poster board to the wall above the bathtub. Draw the outline to the front of a castle on the poster board and leave the rest blank, so your child can color it and add to the kingdom as she sees fit.

Royal Trunk and Contents

The Royal Trunk can be very small, very big, or somewhere in between. Get a cardboard box with a lid that you can wrap, paint, or decorate as a Royal Trunk. The Trunk's contents can be purchased, made, improvised, or imagined.

Beads: Strands of colorful beads that can be worn as necklaces or bracelets and used as decorations.

Princess Cape

Tiara

Crystal Goblet

TREATS TRAY

Drinks

Princess Punch

¾ cup fruit juice

¼ cup carbonated water, mineral water, or clear soda

Serve from the Princess's Crystal Goblet, pretty tea cups, or other fancy unbreakable glasses.

Pink Parasol

1 cup strawberry flavored milk, soymilk, or rice milk

With your child, pretend you are holding a pink parasol and twirl around one time. Then enjoy the drink.

Sparkling Water

1 or 2 ounces of soda

Serve in clear plastic champagne or wineglasses and make a toast before drinking.

Ballroom Bubbles

2 ounces prune juice

1 ounce of cola

Mix well. Great for kids who tend to be constipated.

Hold hands with your child and waltz around the room after drinking the Ballroom Bubbles.

Edible Treats

Finger Sandwiches: two 1-inch-wide cubes of peanut butter and jelly sandwiches

Melon Ice: one or two marble-sized balls of chilled melon with a spoonful of frozen yogurt on top

Ribbon Curls: ⅛ cup long, very thin carrot slices made by using a vegetable peeler

Apple Crisp: 1 teaspoon applesauce served on top of one graham cracker

Cheese Ball: 1 tablespoon grated cheese, like mild cheddar or mozzarella, squeezed and rolled together to form a marble-sized ball

Crystal Sticks: two mini (1 inch-long) salted pretzel sticks

Corn Puffs: two pieces of popcorn

Play Treats

Most of these treats can be used during afternoon potty practice to help your child relax while sitting on the potty. Use the treats to keep your child engaged so she is willing to sit on the potty for several minutes at a time, too.

Princess and Royalty Stickers

Enchanted Bubbles: Mini container of bubbles with a wand. The bubbles are a perfect activity for your child while sitting on her potty-chair.

Modeling Clay: Mini container of modeling clay

Crayons

Markers

Colored Chalk

ACTIVITIES

Alternate between the activities listed below, the theme party books, and the potty-training books and videos.

Morning

Throne Covers

Your child can use crayons, markers, and stickers to decorate a few toilet seat covers fit for a princess.

Princess Necklace

Red shoestring licorice

4 marshmallows

4 small cookies with holes

4 pretzels

Use licorice as the necklace string. Tie more than one length together to make a longer necklace. Thread the licorice through the marshmallows, cookies, and pretzels. Let your child eat a few pieces while making the necklace, but then hang up the necklace in a special place for the Big Kid Grand Finale Celebration at the end of the day. When the party is ready to begin, tie the finished necklace around your child's neck and she can eat parts when hungry.

Ballroom Dancing

Put on some waltzing music and dance with your princess. Make sure you both dance with Dolly too!

Carriage Mask

Help your child make a mask to wear while riding in the Royal Carriage. Cut a plain paper plate in half. Hold it up to your child's face (with the flat edge going across her nose and the rounded curve above her head). Gently mark circles on the mask where your child's eyes are.

Lay the mask down on a flat surface and cut out the eye holes. Your child can color the mask with crayons and markers, put stickers on the mask, and maybe even glue on some shiny beads, coins, or colorful feathers. After your child has finished decorating the mask, tape the end of a long-handled plastic spoon to the back side of the mask to be used as a handle.

Afternoon

Potty Practice Activities

All of the following activities are designed to help make your child's experience of sitting on the potty chair both fun and positive.

Coloring the Kingdom

Each time your child uses the potty, she gets to add to the picture of the Royal Kingdom hanging above the Castle Grounds. She may want to draw a horse, flowers, trees, cat, or even a new dress. Or, she may want you to draw things so she can color them.

Make Me Laugh

Take turns being the Court Jester. Make each other laugh by telling jokes and making funny faces and noises.

From the Carriage, I Spy

Your child can put on her Carriage Mask and tell you what she can see while riding along the road looking out the carriage door.

Theme Books

In addition to the potty-training books listed in the Resources:

Kitty Princess and the Newspaper Dress by Emma Carlow and Trevor
Dickenson

As her amused Fairy Godmouse looks on, Kitty Princess rudely orders
people to make her shoes, jewelry, and a dress for the ball, without
even knowing that she is speaking to the wrong people.

The Princess Knight by Cornelia Funke, illustrations by Kerstin Meyer

Violetta, a little princess, is determined to become as big and strong as
her brothers. So she secretly teaches herself to become the bravest
knight in the land.

The Very Smart Pea and the Princess-to-be by Mini Grey

A funny spoof on a beloved fairy tale.

The Princess and the Pizza by Mary Jane Auch

An out-of-work princess applies to become the bride of a prince, but first
she must pass several tests, including a cooking contest.

Good Night, Princess Pruney Toes by Lisa McCourt

With the help of her loyal subject, Sir Daddy, a young girl pretends to
be a princess as she gets ready for bed.

SHOPPING LISTS

Party Room Decorations—The Castle

Ballroom Floor

Tape

Long silver ribbon

Princess Lounge

Waterproof blanket or rug

Pink bedspread or sheet

2 large silver bows

Banquet Table for Three

Fresh flowers

Linen or pretty plastic lacy
tablecloth

China or princess party plates

Crystal or fancy plastic cups

Bathroom (Royal Carriage) Decorations

Carriage Door

Roll of white butcher paper
(or at least enough white
paper to cover the bathroom
door)

Thick black marker
Light blue paint or crayons
Light pink paint or crayons

Princess Vanity

Child's vanity or pink towel
Hair bows and accessories

Makeup
Nail polish

Princess Throne

Sequins, glitter, small
shiny beads
Spray-mount or hot glue
and gun

Floor cloth
Purple paint
Gold paint

Princess Canopy

Disney's Princess Canopy or plain net canopy which you can find in
most bedding departments
Ceiling hooks or cup hooks

Castle Grounds

4–5 pillows in green pillowcases
2–3 pieces of powder blue poster board
Tape or low-tack putty

Royal Trunk and Contents

Cardboard box with lid, suitcase, or real trunk
Princess wrapping paper or paint to decorate trunk
Colorful beads to be worn as necklaces, bracelets, and decorations
Princess cape
Tiara
Crystal goblet

Grocery Store List

1 bottle carbonated water, mineral water, or clear soda
4–6 different fruit juices (apple, grape, cherry, orange, prune, mango, etc.)
1 quart milk, soymilk, or rice milk
Syrup or powder to make chocolate and strawberry milk
1 bottle of your child's favorite soda
1 bottle *each* of cola and prune juice if you want to make Ballroom Bubbles for a child who tends to be constipated
Miniature party cups that hold about 2 ounces

Edible Treats

Peanut butter and jelly
Bread
Favorite melon
Yogurt
1–2 carrots
Applesauce

Graham crackers
Grated mild cheddar
   or mozzarella cheese
Mini pretzel sticks
Corn puffs or popcorn

Play Treats

Princess and royalty stickers
Bubbles
Modeling clay

Crayons
Markers
Colored chalk

Carriage Mask Supplies

White paper plate
Crayons or colored markers
Princess stickers
Glue

Beads, coins, or colorful feathers
Tape
Long-handled plastic spoon

Princess Necklace Supplies

Red shoestring licorice
4 marshmallows

4 small cookies with holes
4 pretzels

Presents and Prizes

Buy a small but significant present for your child from you and each family member, including Grandma and Granddad if they'll be coming to the Grand Finale Big Kid Celebration. Wrap these ahead of time.

Some Ideas:

Princess slippers

Foaming bath bubbles

Diamond (glass or crystal) necklace

Diamond (glass or crystal) earrings

Princess book or video

Be sure to buy and wrap yourself a present as well. Get something that you really want!

Theme 9

Knights of the Round Table

Kneel and be knighted for your brave and loyal service to the king. Mount your horse and patrol the kingdom, practice your sword-fighting skills, and tame a baby dragon. Test your strength and courage at the royal games, where you compete to win the King's Cup. Celebrate with your loyal friends at the feast that the king is throwing in your honor. Theme colors are royal purple and crimson red, with accents in shining silver.

DECORATIONS

Party Room: The Castle and Grounds

Competition Ring

Make the outline of a Competition Ring by taping a long silver ribbon to the floor in as large a circle as possible. Tie red and purple helium balloons around the ring.

Set up chairs for the audience in a semicircle on one side of the ring. Place dolls or stuffed animals in these chairs. Leave two seats empty—one for you and one for Dolly.

Royal Round Table

Cut a large round circle out of beige or brown poster board. Place a drinking glass in the center of the circle and trace it with a medium-point brown marker. Draw another circle, about an inch larger, around the first one. Draw another about two inches larger outside the second circle and continue drawing circles until you reach the outer circumference of the tree trunk. (The idea is to make the tabletop look like it was made from one massive tree trunk.)

Tape this tabletop to a folding table. Make sure the circle is small enough to completely fit on top of the table. Set pewter goblets on the table. Or you can cover candlesticks and coffee mugs with aluminum foil. (You don't have to be able to drink out of the mugs, but it's more fun if you can.) Place an arrangement of fruit in a wooden or silver bowl in the center of the table. (Bananas, seedless grapes, and tangerines or clementines are all good choices.) If you have a silver or brass pitcher, put that on the table too.

Knight's Lounge Chair

Cover the sofa with a waterproof blanket or rug. On top of that, place a red or purple bedspread or sheet. Attach long silver ribbons to each end of the sofa.

Horse Stable: Bathroom Decorations

Stable Door

Cover the outside of the bathroom door with red paper. Using white paint, make the outline of a barn door. It can be as simple as a large rectangle with a vertical line down the center. Above the stable door, draw a circle the size of a dinner paper plate. (This spot is reserved for the royal crest your knight will color and decorate.)

Horse Stall

Cover the bottom of the bathtub with a thin layer of straw, shredded yellow paper, or straw-colored floral grass. Tape brown poster board to the back wall above the tub. Using a black marker, draw horizontal lines on the poster board about one foot apart—turning the poster board into the wooden boards of a horse stall. If you have a toy rocking horse, spring horse, or stick horse, put it in the stall. Otherwise, you and your child can imagine the horse.

Royal Chest and Contents

Get a medium-size cardboard box with a lid. Paint the outside of the box and lid purple and the inside of the box and lid red. Cut a star out of poster board, cover it with aluminum foil, and glue or tape it to the top of the chest lid.

The contents of the Royal Chest can be purchased, made, improvised, or imagined.

Knight's helmet   Traveling pouch
Gloves   Dragon taming dust (paper confetti)
Sword

TREATS TRAY

Drinks

Grog

1 cup milk (cow, goat, soy, or rice) served in a pewter mug

After drinking it, along with your child rub your belly, grin, and say, "Mm, good Grog!"

Strawberry and chocolate flavored milks are a big hit with kids too.

Sweet Cider

¼ cup carbonated water, mineral water, or clear soda
¾ cup fruit juice

Toast to the king and to the other knights.

Sword Sips

2 ounces prune juice
1 ounce of cola

Mix well. Great for kids who tend to be constipated.

Serve with straws. After drinking, you and your child can wage a "civilized" sword fight with the straws, holding them at arm's length so they are a safe distance from your faces.

Edible Treats

King's Coins: two round carrot slices

Banana Boat: one round slice of banana with a dab of peanut butter or yogurt on top

Trail Mix: ⅛ cup dried chopped fruit mixture

Cheese Ball: 1 tablespoon grated cheese, like mild cheddar or mozzarella, squeezed and rolled together to form a marble-sized ball

Melon Cubes: two dice-size cubes of melon

Horse Reins: two pieces of red string licorice

Shields: two potato chips

Play Treats

Most of these treats can be used during afternoon potty practice to help your child relax while sitting on the potty. Use these treats to keep your child engaged so he is willing to sit on the potty for several minutes at a time, too.

Knight, Castle, and Horse Stickers

Baby Dragon: Tiny toy dragon that your Knight can raise

King's Silver: 1 dime

Crayons

Markers

Crazy Straws

ACTIVITIES

Alternate between the activities listed below, the theme party books, and the potty-training books and videos.

Morning

Make a Royal Crest

Use a white paper plate. Your child can use crayons or markers to decorate the plate with any designs and colors that he likes. He can also put stickers on it. Hang the crest above the stable door.

Decorate Your Knight's Pennant

Cut a one-foot-long triangle out of poster board. Your young knight can color and decorate this pennant. Help him tape a chopstick to the back of the pennant's widest end.

Knight's Competition

Today, the king will choose his champion. Your child can test his skills in the competition ring. Count how long he can stand on one foot and cheer like crazy no matter how long (or short) it is. Have him touch his toes, do a tumbling roll, lie flat, roll over sideways, and other motor skills that you know he can do. After the competition, award him the King's Cup. (This can be a plastic cup or mug that's your child's favorite color or a special cup or mug that you know he'll love.)

Round Table Feast

The royal games have been a great success and the king is throwing a feast in honor of his royal knights. Sit at the round table and enjoy the make-believe feast.

Afternoon

Potty Practice Activities

All of the following activities are designed to help make your child's experience of sitting on the potty-chair fun and successful.

Horse Patrol

The knight must ride his horse around the kingdom, from the castle grounds (party room) to the stable (bathroom) many times during the afternoon. Encourage him to ride a stick horse or a make-believe horse, and from time to time volunteer to be the horse.

Dragon Taming

While your child sits on the toilet, pretend you're a dragon that he is responsible for taming. He can give you commands, such as "stand on one foot," and you must obey to the best of your ability. Other commands could be clap your hands, sing a song, tell me a story, stick out your tongue, and so on. If your knight wants to take a turn at being the dragon, by all means let him.

Knight Tales

Sitting around in the horse stable is a great time for knights to tell and hear travel adventures and stories of courage and honor. Tell your knight a story, read him a book, or ask him to tell you a story.

I Spy

This is an imagination version of I Spy. While your child is sitting on the potty-chair, take turns saying what you can spy from atop your horse as you ride around the kingdom. I spy the king riding in his carriage. I spy the cooks making a feast! I spy the baker making a chocolate pudding pie!

No Laughing Matter

The object of this game is to *not* laugh. Take turns making faces at each other and telling jokes until you make the other one crack up laughing. (When it's your child's turn to make you laugh, don't be too hard of a sell.)

Theme Books

In addition to the potty training books listed in the Resources:

The Making of a Knight: How Sir James Earned His Armor by Patrick O'Brien
Story of James's journey during the Middle Ages in England and his adventures leading up to his knighthood at the age of twenty-one.
Herb, the Vegetarian Dragon by Jules Bass
A knight decides that the time has come to rid the forest of all dragons. Herb, the vegetarian dragon, has a better idea.
Chess-Dream in a Garden by Rosemary Sutcliff
The White King—with his queen, bishops, knights, and pawns—faces the Red Horde in a chesslike battle.
Don Quixote and the Windmills by Eric A. Kimmel
Immersed in tales of knights and dragons and sorcerers and damsels in distress, Señor Quexada proclaims himself and

sets out on his first adventure against some windmills that he thinks
are giants.

*Lassie Come-Home: Eric Knight's Original 1938 classic in a New Picture-
Book Edition* by Rosemary Wells, illustrations by Susan Jeffers

Sold in financial desperation to a wealthy duke, a collie undertakes a
1,000-mile journey in order to be reunited with her former master in
Yorkshire.

SHOPPING LISTS

Party Room Decorations

Competition Ring

Tape
Long silver ribbon
4–5 red or purple helium-filled balloons tied to 2–4 feet strings
Chairs
Dolls *or* stuffed animals

Royal Round Table

Large piece of beige or tan poster board
Medium-point brown marker
Pewter goblets (or improvise and cover candlesticks and lightweight cof-
fee mugs or plastic cups with aluminum foil)
Wooden or silver bowl
Assortment of fruit (bananas, seedless grapes, apples, or oranges)
Silver *or* brass pitcher

Knight's Lounge Chair

Waterproof blanket or rug   Several long silver ribbons
Red or purple bedspread or sheet

Bathroom (Horse Stable) Decorations

Stable Door

Red paper (enough to cover bathroom door)
White paint or construction paper
Painter's tape or low-tack putty

Horse Stall

Straw, shredded yellow paper, or beige Easter basket grass
Painter's tape or low-tack putty
Brown paper or poster board
Thick black marker
Toy rocking horse, spring horse, or stick horse

Royal Chest and Contents

Cardboard box with lid
Red and purple paint
Paintbrushes

Star cut out of poster board and
   covered with aluminum foil
Glue or tape

Contents of the royal chest can be purchased, made, improvised, or imagined.

Knight's helmet
Gloves
Sword

Traveling pouch
Dragon taming dust (paper confetti)

Grocery Store List

1 bottle of carbonated water, mineral water, or clear soda
4–6 different fruit juices (apple, grape, cherry, orange, prune,
   mango, etc.)
1 quart milk, soymilk, or rice milk
Syrup or powder to make chocolate and strawberry milk
1 bottle of your child's favorite soda
1 bottle each of cola and prune juice if you want to make Sword Sips for
   a child who tends to be constipated
Miniature party cups that hold about 2 ounces

Edible Treats

1–2 carrots

1–2 bananas

Peanut butter or favorite
 yogurt

Trail mix or dried chopped
 fruit mixtures

Grated mild cheddar or
 mozzarella cheese

Favorite melon

Red string licorice

Potato chips

Play Treats

Knight, castle, and horse stickers

Tiny toy dragon (child can raise)

1 dime

Crayons

Markers

Crazy straws

Morning activity supply list

White paper plate

1 piece poster board (to cut a 1-foot-long triangle)

Decorative cup or mug in your child's favorite color

Presents and Prizes

Buy a small but significant present for your child from you and each family member, including Grandma and Granddad if they'll be coming to the Grand Finale Big Kid Celebration. Wrap these ahead of time.

Some Ideas:

Knight's armor

Boots

Knee pads

Book or video about self-esteem and courage

Sign for bedroom door that reads: "The Knight (and your Child's
 first name)"

Buy and wrap yourself a present too! Make sure it's worthy of a queen!

Theme 10

Incredibly Cool Camp-Out

Take off your backpack, pitch your tent, and gather 'round the fire ring for story swapping and s'mores. When you're ready for adventure, climb into the secret clubhouse and grab the trail map. Follow the map to find hidden treasures in the camp ground, the clubhouse, and everywhere in between! Theme colors are forest green, burnt orange, and berry red.

DECORATIONS

Party Room: Camp Ground

Camp Site

Pitch a small tent or improvise one with a large blanket or bedspread draped over a few chairs. If your child has a sleeping bag, put it in the tent. If not, put a pillow and blanket inside the tent.

Fire Ring

If you have a real fireplace and it's cold enough for a fire, get your kindling ready and build it ahead of time so all you have to do is light it and keep it going during the party. Real fires are perfect for making s'mores. If you don't have a fireplace or it's too warm for a fire, improvise. Put a small brown rug or towel on the floor. Cover the edge of the rug or towel with large river rocks. (If you don't have easy access to river rocks, you can use any large stones or crumble balls of brown construction or packing paper for rocks.) To make a fire, put some shredded orange, yellow, and red paper in the center of the ring.

Forest Clearing

Lay a green tarp on the floor. Tape the four corners of the tarp to the floor or weigh them down with artificial potted plants or spill-proof real ones (if they exist). Firmly tape coloring book pictures of forest animals on the tarp. Deer, raccoons, squirrels, rabbits, birds, turtles, and any and all of your child's favorites.

Night Sky

Glow in the dark stars have to be a part of this! Attach them to the walls and the ceiling.

Decorating tip from Matt and Shari of *Room by Room* on HGTV

Secret Clubhouse: Bathroom Decorations

Clubhouse Door

Cover the outside of the bathroom door with white paper. Paint or use a fat marker to draw a big tree trunk from the bottom of the door up about two feet. On top of the tree trunk, draw a door that is just large enough for your child to crawl through. Draw tree branches around the door. Write the words "Secret Clubhouse" on the door.

The Tree Room

Put a green slip-proof rug or mat in the bathtub or on the shower stall floor. Take down the shower curtain or tie it together at one end of the curtain rod. Hang brown streamers from the curtain rod to about three inches above the floor. The streamers will form a loose curtain that your child can step through. Tape green leaves made out of construction paper or purchased from a craft store onto the streamers at varying heights. Put two or three leaves on each streamer to give the effect of standing up in the branches of a tree.

Look-Out Post

Hang a sign on the wall next to or behind the potty chair that says "Look-Out Post." If you find a picture of binoculars in a magazine or can draw them, put them on the sign. Place a small sketchbook and crayons or markers in a magazine rack next to the potty-chair.

Backpack and Contents

You can use a real child-size backpack or decorate a paper grocery bag that has handles. The contents of the backpack can be purchased, made, improvised, or imagined.

Binoculars

Magnifying glass

Compass

Treasure map

Flashlight

Water bottle or canteen

TREATS TRAY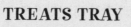

Drinks

Cool Break

Use juice boxes in a variety of flavors.

Sit next to your child and describe the imaginary view you see as you drink your juice boxes.

Chocolate Malt or Berry Blast

Mix milk (dairy, soy, or rice) with chocolate or strawberry flavoring and serve in tall plastic cups or mugs

White Water

¾ cup white grape juice

¼ cup mineral or sparkling water

Mix well. Together with your child, pretend you are paddling a raft after finishing your drink.

Moose Juice

2 ounces prune juice

1 ounce of cola

Great for kids who tend to be constipated.

Mix well. After drinking the juice, walk on your hands and knees with your child, pretending to be moose.

Edible Treats

Mini-Dog: 1-inch slice of beef, turkey, or soy dog on a plastic fork, served plain or with ketchup

Cheese Cubes: two dice-size pieces of your child's favorite cheese

Trail Mix: a few teaspoons of dried fruits and/or nuts

Fish: two fish-shaped crackers

Sticks: two thin salted pretzel sticks

Stones: two nuts or pitted black olives

Safety Rope: one strand of red licorice

Camping Burger: two round crackers with a slice of heated meatball in between

If you don't want your child to eat treats made with refined sugar, check out the options available in health food stores.

Play Treats

Most of these treats can be used during afternoon potty practice to help your child relax while sitting on the potty. Use the treats to keep him engaged so he is willing to sit on the potty for several minutes at a time, too.

Stickers: Camping, forest animals and birds, other nature themes

Crazy Straws

Magic Sponges

Biodegradable (flushable) miniature sponges that expand into shapes when they're wet.

Fish Bubbles: Mini container of bubbles with a bubble wand. Bubbles are a great activity for your child while sitting on his potty-chair.

ACTIVITIES

Alternate between the activities listed below, the theme party books, and the potty-training books and videos.

Morning

Hiking & Exploring

Your child is in charge of leading today's expedition through the house and around the yard if the weather is nice. The reason for today's hike is to show Dolly all of the rooms in the house and the fun spots in the yard. You tag along while your child gives Dolly a guided tour.

Want S'more?

Toast a marshmallow over a gas or electric burner (or in a fireplace if you have a fire going). When the marshmallow is light brown, place it on top of a graham cracker and place a piece of chocolate and another graham cracker on top. If your child wants to make more than one, save the others for the party at the end of the day. They can be reheated in the oven or in a toaster oven.

Old-Fashioned Popcorn

Remember when Jiffy Pop was like space-age technology? Whoa . . . We all breathed in unison as we watched the pop-top rise. In today's age of microwave popcorn, Jiffy Pop is a blast from the past.

Veggie Forest

Fresh carrots, beets, and parsnips
Shallow plastic plate
Small plastic animals
Small stones and pebbles

Select 4–5 vegetables with little or no foliage. Cut them 1 to 2 inches from the top. Discard or cook the lower portions. Place the tops in the plate and pour in a little water. Place the plate on a sunny window ledge. In a few days green shoots will appear. Keep water in the plate. Arrange pebbles and toy animals amongst the sprouting vegetables to make a forestlike environment.

Afternoon

Potty Practice Activities

All of the following activities are designed to help make your child's experience of going to the bathroom and sitting on the potty-chair fun and successful.

Treasure Hunt

Nature's treasures are hidden in the campground, the secret club-house, and everywhere in between. Your child can follow the trail map and your spoken clues to find each treasure. Hide three to seven treasures like pretty stones, feathers, colorful leaves, interesting sea shells, pine cones, etc. Every time he finds one, he gets to take it to the secret clubhouse, store it in the tree room, and sit on the look-out post to spy on the rest of the campground.

Story Swapping

Ask your child to tell you all about the best camping trip he can imagine. Who would go on the trip with him? What would they do? What would they eat? Who would cook? Who would wash the dishes? When he finishes his story, you tell him one or read him one.

I Spy a Forest Friend

While your child is sitting on his look-out post, he can use his binoculars (or pretend binoculars) to play I Spy a Forest Friend. He can name different animals and birds that he might see and tell you what they look like. When he gets off the potty, he gets to color one of the forest friends on the forest clearing in the party room.

Chasing Away the Clouds

Fill up a few large white balloons with air. When you want your child to make his way to the bathroom, race him by calling out the name of the game: Let's Chase the Clouds Away!

You both pick a balloon and race to the bathroom by kicking or pushing the balloon in front of you. You and your child can use anything to move the balloon forward and into the clubhouse except your hands.

Theme Books

In addition to the potty-training books and videos listed in the Resources:

Let's Go Camping with Mr. Sillypants by M. K. Brown
When Mr. Sillypants gets lost on a camping trip, he has a dream about the Three Bears.

Angelina and Henry by Katharine Holabird, illustrations by Helen Craig
While on a camping trip, two young mice become lost until the fit and fearless Angelina saves the day.

Acorn Magic by Maggie Stern, pictures by Donna Ruff
Mrs. Potter takes Simon camping to look for birds, but even though he brings along his magic acorn the trip doesn't turn out the way he expected.

Whistling by Elizabeth Partridge, drawings by Anna Grossnickle Hines
While on a camping trip with his father, a boy draws on the whistling practice they have shared and finally whistles up the sun.

Frank and Izzy Set Sail by Laura McGee Kvasnosky
Frank the bear and Izzy the rabbit sail to Crescent Island and camp overnight.

SHOPPING LISTS

Party Room Decorations

Camp Site

Small tent or blanket or bedspread over chairs
Sleeping bag or pillow and blanket (for inside tent)
Glow in the dark stars

Fire Ring

Kindling wood (if you have a real fireplace)
Or small brown rug or towel

Large river rocks, large stones, or crumbled balls of brown construction
  or packing paper
Shredded orange, yellow, and red paper

Forest Clearing

Green tarp or plastic picnic tablecloth
Potted plant containers (real or artificial)
Pictures of forest animals (deer, racoons, squirrels, rabbits, birds, turtles,
  and other favorites)

Bathroom (Secret Clubhouse) Decorations

Clubhouse Door

Roll of white butcher paper (or at least enough white paper to cover the
  bathroom door)
Paint or fat markers, brown and green

The Tree Room

Green slip-proof rug or mat
Brown streamer paper
5–10 pieces green construction paper to make leaves (or purchase from
  a craft store)
(If it's fall, tape or staple real fallen leaves to the streamers.)

Look-Out Post

White poster board or construction paper
Painter's tape or low-tack putty
Picture of binoculars cut from camping magazine
Small sketch book
Crayons or package of washable markers
Magazine rack

Backpack and Contents

Child-size backpack, or a paper grocery bag with handles

The contents of the backpack can be purchased, made, improvised, or imagined.

Binoculars	Treasure map
Magnifying glass	Flashlight
Compass	Water bottle or canteen

Grocery Store List

1 bottle of carbonated water, mineral water, or clear soda

4–6 different fruit juice boxes (apple, grape, cherry, orange, prune, mango, etc.)

Milk, soymilk, or rice milk in single service containers

Syrup or powder to make chocolate and strawberry milk

1 bottle of white grape juice

1 bottle each of cola and prune juice if you want to make Moose Juice for a child who tends to be constipated

Miniature party cups that hold about 2 ounces

Edible Treats

Beef, turkey, or soy hotdog	Round crackers
Package of your child's favorite cubed cheese	Miniature meatballs
	Marshmallows
Dried fruits and/or nuts	Graham crackers
Fish-shaped crackers	Chocolate bar
Mini salted pretzel sticks	Jiffy Pop popcorn
Favorite nuts and/or pitted black olives	Fresh carrots, beets, and parsnips with tops still attached
Red string licorice	(will use to make veggie forest)

Play Treats

Stickers in camping, forest animals and birds, or other nature themes

Crazy straws

Flushable (biodegradable) potty targets (see Resources)

Bubbles

Activity Supply List

Miniature plastic toy animals and pebbles (will use to make veggie forest)

Treasure hunt supplies: pretty stones, feathers, colorful leaves, interesting seashells, pinecones, etc.

Large white balloons for chasing away the clouds

Presents and Prizes

Buy a small but significant present for your child from you and each family member, including Grandma and Granddad if they'll be coming to the Grand Finale Big Kid Celebration. Wrap these ahead of time.

Some Ideas:

Sleeping bag	Hiking boots or sports shoes
Indoor tent	Walking stick
Kid-size cooler	Weekend pass for a real camp-out

Buy and wrap a present for yourself, too, or assign this support task to your partner or a willing friend or relative.

Theme 11
All Aboard Train Trip

All aboard! Make your own engineer hat, catch a movie in the lounge, and try your luck at a new card game. Visit the dining car for a drink and a snack. Treat yourself to a foot massage, make spice clay creations, and enjoy the view from your private cabin. Theme colors are deep rose, slate gray, and warm yellow.

DECORATIONS

Party Room: The Train

The Game Room

Set up a small table or a round rug on the floor. This is the area where people on the train gather to play games.

The Dining Car

A bench, love seat, or three chairs set up in front of a folding table covered with a plastic tablecloth. If it's easy to do, arrange the furniture so that there's a real window at the end of the bench. Otherwise, put up a piece of poster board with a drawing of a window.

The Lounge

This is the car where you will go to read, watch potty-training videos, and relax. Cover your sofa with a waterproof blanket, rug, or tarp. Place a colored sheet, blanket, or bedspread on top.

Private Cabin: Bathroom Decorations

Cabin Door

Cover the bathroom door with light gray paper. Draw a child-size door in the center of the paper. You can make the top of the cabin door a semicircle or a straight line. Draw a peephole at your child's eye level. Draw a keyhole below the doorknob at a height your child can easily reach.

Hide-Away Bed

Put sofa pillows or outdoor furniture pillows in the bathtub. Securely tape or staple two large sheets of poster board together. Lay the poster board on top of the pillow bed. Set some books on top.

Travel Closet

Hang a few of your child's favorite outfits and a favorite coat on the shower curtain rod.

Moving View

Draw a window on a piece of powder blue poster board. Paint or color the bottom of the window with grass. Paint or color some white clouds on the blue sky. Hang this window next to the potty-chair.

Train Trunk and Contents

Paint or cover a medium-size box and lid with poster board or construction paper. Decorate the box to look like a train trunk. Put a label on one side of the trunk with your child's name and address. The contents of the train trunk can be purchased, made, improvised, or imagined.

Cabin Key: a large toy plastic key
Train Whistle: a whistle that sounds like a train
Binoculars
Sketch Pad
Color Pencils or Markers
Age-Appropriate Games such as Candy Land, Chutes and Ladders, and Hi Ho! Cherry-O
Red Bandana

TREATS TRAY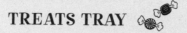

Drinks

Grape Spritzer

¾ cup grape juice (use white grape juice if you're worried about spills)

¼ cup carbonated water, mineral water, or clear soda

You can also make Cherry Spritzer or any other fruit flavor your child enjoys.

While drinking your spritzers, take turns naming things you can see from the train window.

Choo-Choo Milk Shake Made to Order

1 cup of milk (the flavor your child likes best)

½ cup ice cream

Mix in blender. After drinking, say "Choo-choo, Choo-choo. Choo-choo, Choo-choo. Wooa-woo!"

Soda Fizz

2 ounces of soda measured out into a cup

Fast Track

2 ounces prune juice

1 ounce of cola

Mix well. Great for kids who tend to be constipated.

After your child drinks the Fast Track, race her to her private cabin (bathroom) and back.

Edible Treats

Peanut Butter Finger: a ½-inch-wide slice of a peanut butter and jelly sandwich with no crust

Cheese Wheel: a round slice of cheese on a round cracker

Fruit Cup: one or two berries, melon balls, and/or apple slices served in a teacup

Surf & Turf: one fish-shaped cracker and one animal cracker

Pudding Pie: one teaspoon of pudding or yogurt on a graham cracker. (If you want to get really fancy, put a tiny dab or squirt of whipped cream on top.)

Chips & Dip: two potato or corn chips with a teaspoon of dip

Pretzel Rings: two salted pretzel rings

Candy Bar Bite: ½-inch-thick slice of your child's favorite candy bar

If you don't want your child to eat treats made with refined sugar, check out the alternatives available in health food stores.

Play Treats

Most of these treats can be used during afternoon potty practice to help your child relax while sitting on the potty. Use the treats to keep your child engaged so he is willing to sit on the potty for several minutes at a time, too.

Train Stickers or stickers of things you might see from a train window

Crazy Straws

Engine Bubbles: Mini container of bubbles with a bubble wand. (Before the water turns to steam in the engine, it bubbles.) Bubbles are a great activity for your child while sitting on his potty-chair.

Train-Shaped Expandable Sponges: biodegradable (flushable) sponges that puff up to look like trains when they're wet (see Resources)

ACTIVITIES

Alternate between the activities listed below, the theme party books, and the potty-training books and videos.

Morning

Make Spice Clay

½ cup applesauce

½ cup flour

¼ cup cinnamon

¼ cup nutmeg

¼ cup white glue

Measure and mix these ingredients with your child and store them in the refrigerator for the afternoon.

Engineer's Hat

Black poster board

Safety scissors

Clear tape

Cut a piece of poster board 2- or 3-inches high and about 1 foot long. Curve the piece into a circle and fit on top of your child's head. Close the circle and tape it so that the hat rim sits snugly on your child's head.

Place the hat rim on the remaining poster board. Draw a circle all the way around the rim of the hat about one-inch larger than the rim. Cut out this circle and tape it inside the hat rim. Set the hat rim and top on the poster board once more. Draw a crescent shaped hat visor on the poster board, cut it out, and staple or tape to the bottom of the hat rim.

Snacks in the Dining Car

Select a treat for Dolly and for yourself and invite your child to select a treat and drink for himself. Relax in the dining car while enjoying your refreshments. Discuss the imaginary scenery that the train is passing.

A Game of Chance

Teach your child how to play the new game in his train trunk, and play it together in the dining car or in the lounge.

Afternoon

Potty Practice Activities

Most of the following activities are designed to help make your child's experience of sitting on the potty-chair both fun and positive.

Spice Clay Creations

Take the spice clay out of the refrigerator. Your child can knead it, play with it, and mold it while sitting on his potty-chair.

Blowing Engine Bubbles

Imagine you are helping the Little Engine that Could. Blow bubbles to help the train engine work better and make more steam.

Steam Shapes

Look for and name the imaginary shapes on the ceiling above the potty-chair that the train engine is making.

Salon Treatment

Give your child a manicure or a pedicure while he's sitting on the potty. The nail polish is optional.

Hand or Foot Massage

Use some lotion and give your child a foot massage or a hand massage while he sits on the potty-chair.

I Spy This Picture

Using the sketch pad and a pencil or marker, your child can draw the pictures that he sees out of his train window while sitting on the potty-chair.

Sing

Sing songs like "I've Been Working on the Railroad" and "The Wheels on the Train Go Round and Round." Have fun making up new words and verses.

Theme Books

In addition to the potty training books listed in the Resources:

This Train by Paul Collicutt
Simple text and illustrations depict different kinds of trains going over

hills, crossing bridges and tunnels, using electric or steam, and carrying passengers or freight, even when it snows.

Train Song by Harriet Ziefert and paintings by Donald Saaf
Rhyming storybook of a young boy watching a freight train go on its daily run.

I Knew You Could! by Craig Dorfman
The Little Engine That Could advises how to find one's own track in life.

Crossing by Philip Booth, illustrated by Bagram Ibatoulline
Illustrations and text capture the rhythm and motion of a moving freight train.

Thomas and Friends: Percy's Chocolate Crunch and other Thomas the Tank Engine Stories by David Milton, illustrations based on *The Railway Series* by the Rev. W. Awdry
A collection of stories about Percy, Harold the Helicopter, and other friends of Thomas the Tank Engine.

SHOPPING LISTS

Party Room Decorations—The Train

The Game Room

Small table or round rug on floor

The Dining Car

A bench, love seat, or three chairs
Folding table

Plastic tablecloth
Piece of poster board
Painter's tape or low-tack putty

The Lounge

Waterproof blanket, rug, or tarp
Colored sheet, blanket, or bedspread

Bathroom (Private Cabin) Decorations

Cabin Door

Light gray paper (enough to cover the bathroom door)
Thick black marker

Hide-Away Bed

Sofa pillows or outdoor lounge chair pillows
Two large sheets of poster board

Moving View

Powder blue poster board   White paint or crayons
Green paint or crayons   Painter's tape or low-tack putty

Train Trunk and Contents

Cover a medium-size box and lid with paint, poster board, or construction paper.

Contents of the Train Trunk can be purchased, made, improvised, or imagined.

Cabin key   Color pencils or markers
Train whistle   Age-appropriate card game
Binoculars   Red bandana
Sketch pad

Grocery Store List

1 bottle of carbonated water, mineral water, or clear soda
4–6 different fruit juices (apple, grape, cherry, orange, prune, mango, etc.)
1 quart milk, soymilk, or rice milk
Syrup or powder to make chocolate and strawberry milk
1 bottle of your child's favorite soda
1 bottle each of cola and prune juice if you want to make Fast Tracks for a child who tends to be constipated
Miniature party cups that hold about 2 ounces

Edible Treats

Peanut butter and jelly sandwich
Favorite cheese slices and round crackers
Favorite berries, melon, and/or apple slices
Fish-shaped and animal crackers
Favorite flavor pudding, yogurt, and/or whipped cream
Graham crackers
Potato or corn chips and favorite dip
Small bag of miniature pretzel rings
1 candy bar

Play Treats

Train stickers
Crazy straws
Bubbles

Flushable (biodegradable)
   potty targets (see Resources)

Activity Supply List

Applesauce, flour, cinnamon,
   nutmeg, and white glue

Black poster board
Clear tape

Presents and Prizes

Buy a small but significant present for your child from you and each family
member, including Grandma and Granddad if they'll be coming to the
Grand Finale Big Kid Celebration. Wrap these ahead of time.

Some Ideas:

Small train engine or train set
Engineer's suspenders
Engineer's bib overalls
Tickets to go on a train ride (these can be real tickets for a local train
   ride, an amusement park train, or a miniature train village, or make
   tickets for a play or pretend train ride)
Book or video of a train adventure
Buy and wrap a present for yourself too!

Theme 12

Cartoon Character Carnival

Your favorite cartoon character has arrived at your door, toting a suitcase of surprises. Get ready for excitement because you have funny things to say, silly games to play, pictures to take, and cool stuff to make! To change yourself into your cartoon character, run, skip, hop, roll, slither, or crawl into the changing room! Theme colors are particular colors associated with your child's favorite character. Otherwise, use your child's favorite colors.

DECORATIONS

Party Room: TV Land

Wall-to-Wall Fun

Spread a tarp or floor cloth on the floor. If possible, secure the tarp to the floor with painter's tape to keep it from sliding. Cut several pictures of the cartoon character out of coloring books, magazines, greeting cards, or calendars. Arrange these on the tarp and firmly attach them using clear tape around the entire picture.

Toddler-Size Cut-Out

Draw the character on a large piece of white foam board and cut it out. Lean the cut-out against a wall, table, or chair. (You can also glue a life-size poster of the character to a piece of foam board instead of drawing it, and then cut it out.)

Character Combo

Gather everything your child owns that's related to the theme's cartoon character. You can cover a sofa in the party room with character-theme sheets, a bedspread, or a comforter. Put pictures and posters of the character and his or her sidekicks on the walls. Set character dolls and related toys, books, and games around the party room.

Changing Room: Bathroom Decorations

Changing Room Door

Cover the outside of the bathroom door with aluminum foil or reflective silver wrapping paper. Using a marker, draw the outline of your child's hands about six inches apart (and at her shoulder height) on the door. Above the hand outlines, tape a picture of your child's favorite cartoon character. Below the hands, tape a picture of your child.

Put stickers of your child's favorite cartoon character all over the door.

Double the Fun

Tape a photo of your child onto the mirror next to a picture of the cartoon character.

Character Kitsch

Lots of cartoon characters adorn a variety of products from soap and toothpaste dispensers to shower curtains, towels, and toilet paper. You can also use theme stickers, streamers, ribbons, and bows to turn any object into one of the party decorations.

Potty Tent

Lots of the popular cartoon characters like Spider-Man and Sponge-Bob have pop-up tents that are big enough for a potty-chair to fit inside. If you use the tent like this, use a clothes pin to hold open the tent door. If your bathroom isn't big enough to comfortably accommodate a pop-up tent, place one in the party room or skip the tent entirely.

Cartoon Character Suitcase and Contents

Use a real suitcase (one you already own or a new one for your child) or make a suitcase out of a large paper shopping bag with handles. Paint the bag or cover the outside of it with construction paper. Decorate with character theme stickers.

The contents of the suitcase can be purchased, made, improvised, imagined, or improvised.

Theme character T-shirt
Hat, helmet, or other headgear
Character's belt, tools, or equipment
Crayons or washable markers

TREATS TRAY

Drinks

Just Juice

If you can find juice boxes or other containers with the cartoon character featured, that's an added bonus. Your child can pretend he is his favorite character drinking the juice.

Funny Fizzy

¾ cup fruit juice
¼ cup carbonated water, mineral water, or clear soda
    Serve in a plastic cup decorated with theme character stickers. Encourage your child to do something her favorite character does that she thinks is funny.

Take Two

¾ cup milk (dairy, soy, or rice)
¼ cup ice cream or frozen yogurt (soy or rice)
    Mix in a blender. Use your child's favorite flavors. After your child drinks the shake he "turns into" his favorite character and acts out a scene.

Power Pop

2 ounces prune juice
1 ounce of cola

Mix well. Great for kids who tend to be constipated.
After drinking Power Pop, your child pretends she is ten times
stronger.

Edible Treats

Carrot Curls: ⅛ cup of thin carrot slices

Banana Bites: 1-inch slice of banana with a dab of peanut butter
or yogurt

Applesauce: ¼ cup applesauce

Cheese Cubes: two dice-size pieces of cheese

Chips & Dip: two potato chips with 1 teaspoon dip

M&Ms: one or two

Pretzels: one or two small pretzels

If you don't want your child to eat treats made with refined sugar, check out the options available in health
food stores.

Play Treats

Most of these treats can be used during afternoon potty practice to
help your child relax while sitting on the potty. Use the treats to keep your
child engaged so she is willing to sit on the potty for several minutes at a
time, too.

Magic Sponges: Biodegradable (flushable) miniature sponges that expand into shapes when they're wet.

Theme Character Stickers

Theme Character Jewelry or Badges

Crazy Straws

ACTIVITIES

Alternate between the activities listed below, the theme party books, and
the potty-training books and videos.

Morning

Greatest Hits

Your child can act out her favorite cartoon character scenes and moments and make up her own story lines. She can also play the role of the director giving acting instructions to you and Dolly.

Cartoon Art

Your child can color the coloring book pictures you've taped to the floor cover or tarp. She can also add stickers to the covering and use markers or crayons to add her own artistic touches.

Cartoon Character Coasters

four 4-inch-wide clear plastic circles*	Pencil
four 4-inch-wide circles of felt	Felt tip marker
four coaster-size pictures of favorite cartoon characters	Scissors
	Spray mount
	Glue

These coasters—made from original art, photos, or a combination of both—are fun to make and fun to use.

Place one of the plastic circles over a picture, "framing" it the way you want the coaster to look. Hold the circle in place and trace it with a pencil. Cut out the photo and set aside. Place the plastic circle on a piece of felt and use a felt tip marker to trace it. Cut out the felt circle and glue it to the back of your picture. Next, spray the front of the picture with spray mount and press the plastic circle on top.

*The ¼-inch-thick plastic circles are available at home improvement stores like Home Depot or Lowe's, or at Industrial Plastic Supply Co. (www.yourplasticsupermarket.com)

Afternoon

Potty Practice Activities

Most of the following activities are designed to help make your child's experience of sitting on the potty-chair both fun and positive.

Character Changes

When your child wants to change into the character or back into herself, she will do it in the Changing Room. You can suggest the changes when you feel your child might be ready to urinate or have a bowel movement. "Come on Ellie, let's race to the changing room. It's time for you to change back into (name of character). Hurry. Hurry. Dolly needs you!" Or something like that.

Character References

Take turns saying what you think is great about her favorite cartoon character. Then take turns saying what her favorite character probably thinks is great about her. And last, but not least, take turns telling what you think is great about each other.

Story Lines

Read books and tell each other stories. The stories can be real or made up.

Photo Shoot

Temporarily bend the head of the toddler-size cartoon character cut-out down and tape it to the character's back. Each time your child sits on the potty, she gets to have a photo taken behind the cut-out. (She can make different faces in the photos or do the same thing in every one. Her choice.)

Arrange for a phone call from the cartoon character or his or her Mom congratulating your child for potty training her doll.

Theme Books

In addition to the potty-training books listed in the Resources:

Adventures of Sparrow Boy by Brian Pinkney
After an encounter with sparrow, Henry finds he is able to fly just like his favorite comic book hero HawkMan.

Your Dog Plays Hockey? by Charles M. Schulz
The adventures of the Peanuts gang.
Look for any other books related to your child's favorite cartoon
   characters.

SHOPPING LISTS

Party Room Decorations—TV Land

Wall-to-Wall Fun

Waterproof tarp or floor cloth (remnant piece of cartoon fabric or top
   sheet from cartoon bedding)
Several pictures of cartoon character
Clear tape (if you want to permanently attach, cover with contact
   paper)

Toddler-Size Cut-Out

Roll of white butcher paper (or at least enough white paper to draw a
   toddler-size cartoon cut-out)
Glue or tape
Two pieces of cardboard attached, or one large toddler-size piece of
   cardboard
Life-size poster of cartoon character

Character Combo

Everything your child owns that's cartoon-theme related: sheets,
   bedspread, comforter, pictures, posters, dolls, toys, books, and
   games

Bathroom (Changing Room) Decorations

Two boxes of aluminum foil or reflective silver wrapping paper
Thick black marker
Picture of your child's favorite cartoon character
Clear tape
Cartoon stickers

Double the Fun

Photo of your child and cartoon character (comparable in size)
Clear or painter's tape

Character Kitsch

   Cartoon character bathroom accessories: soap and toothpaste dispensers, toothbrush and toothbrush holder, comb and hairbrush, shower curtain, towels, throw rugs, hand towels, and bath toys
   Cartoon theme stickers, streamers, ribbons, and bows

Cartoon Character Suitcase and Contents

Real suitcase (one you already own or a new theme suitcase) or large
   paper shopping bag with handles
Paint or construction paper
Theme stickers

   Contents of the Suitcase can be purchased, made, improvised, or imagined.

Theme character T-shirt
Hat, helmet, or other head gear
Character's belt, tools, or equipment
Crayons or washable markers

Grocery Store List

   4–6 different fruit juice boxes (apple, grape, cherry, orange, prune, mango, etc.)
   1 bottle of carbonated water, mineral water, or clear soda
   1 bottle of your child's favorite fruit juice
   1 quart of milk, soymilk, or rice milk
   1 small container ice cream or frozen yogurt (soy or rice)
   1 bottle each of cola and prune juice if you want to make Power Pop
      for a child who tends to be constipated
   Miniature party cups that hold about 2 ounces

Edible Treats

1–2 carrots and bananas

Peanut butter or favorite yogurt

Applesauce in single serving
    package

Favorite type of cheese

Potato chips

Favorite dip

Small bag of M&Ms

Small bag of miniature pretzels

Play Treats

Flushable (biodegradable) potty targets (see Resources)

Theme character stickers

Theme character jewelry or badges

Crazy straws

Activity Supply List

four 4-inch clear plastic circles

four 4-inch circles of felt

four coaster-size pictures of
    favorite cartoon characters

Pencil or felt tip marker

Scissors

Spray mount

Glue

Presents and Prizes

Buy a small but significant present for your child from you and each family member, including Grandma and Granddad if they'll be coming to the Grand Finale Big Kid Celebration. Wrap these ahead of time.

Some Ideas:

Cartoon character outfit

Cartoon character hat, belt, ring, or other accessory

Coloring book featuring the cartoon character

New cartoon character movie

Picture or poster of cartoon character

> You get a present too. At least one. Buy yourself one or two things that you'd really like to have and wrap them for the party.

7. all you need to know to become a potty pro

Which rooms are best for the potty party?

The living room or family room and the bathroom.

What should my demeanor be like during the potty party?

You most definitely want to exude enthusiasm and act like you're having a lot of fun during the potty party. Use a lot of positive reinforcement. Congratulate your child on all her successes. Give hugs, high-fives (hand slaps), and kisses. Dance around the room in excitement—your child will eat up your undivided attention.

What type of snacks should I provide?

Be sure to have a wide assortment. I suggest a variety of cookies, potato chips, dried fruit, sweetened cereal, and pretzels, and there are some great treat ideas in the party themes section of chapter six. Kids really seem to love M&Ms and Reese's Pieces, but it's important to have a balance of party snacks and healthy treats like fruit. (A lot of parents use organic products.) Remember you are offering bite-size morsels, not whole Twinkies or cupcakes. I had a lot of treats on hand, but my son Spencer preferred M&Ms over anything else I offered him. Even though he chose an M&M treat most frequently, by the end of the day, he'd only eaten about a dozen M&Ms. You really need to keep quantity in perspective. Remember, less is more when offering treats.

Do I need to use all the recommended steps or can I eliminate the ones my child seems to already have mastered?

If your child is "half trained," meaning he sometimes urinates in the potty but always has BMs in his diaper, you'll still need to follow all the potty party prerequisites and training steps. However, you can reduce the amount of time you spend on certain steps if your child demonstrates that he has mastered them. If you feel your child really has a handle on training the doll to urinate after just an hour or so into the potty party, give more time to discussing and demonstrating BMs with the doll. During the afternoon part of the party, though, you will still need to encourage your child to eat and drink to give him the opportunity to reinforce his success/consistency on the potty.

How will I know for sure if my child has the bladder capacity for a potty party?

If you notice she urinates large amounts at one time and can stay dry for the hours in between each wet diaper change, she is probably ready.

How can I be certain my child can follow all the instructions during the potty party?

Give your child this simple test to see if he can follow directions: 1. touch his hair or head, 2. clap his hands, 3. sit on a chair, 4. walk with you to the bathroom, 5. point to his nose or face, 6. touch his legs or arms, 7. play patty-cake with you, 8. throw or roll you a ball, 9. pick out a book to read, 10. bring you a toy, and 11. point to his shoes or feet. If he can follow eight to ten of these instructions, he's most likely intellectually ready to be potty trained.

What if my child is very stubborn or prone to temper tantrums—will a potty party work?

Many children who are stubborn or have temper tantrums do so because they do not feel like they are in control of their situation or because they are trying to get more attention. That's why a potty party is perfect for this type of child—they get to control the morning part of the party by being the teacher, plus, they are the center of positive attention in both the morning and the afternoon.

What is the best way to prepare a child for potty training?

Begin by modeling the behavior for him. Allow your child to watch you, your spouse, and other siblings use the toilet. Explain what you are doing on the toilet and teach him potty vocabulary, how to raise and lower his pants, and how to wash his hands.

If I was unsuccessful in earlier attempts to toilet train my child, should I have someone else try it this time?

That depends. If your child had a very negative response to your earlier training method and is fearful or extremely resistant to toilet training, then I would strongly suggest you find a Potty-Training Pinch Hitter. See chapter two for suggestions. If, however, he was just uninterested or perhaps not ready the last time you tried, I'd say give it another shot. If you're in the middle of training and it's not going well or your child is crying, stop! Try a few months later or pass the potty-training baton to a spouse, relative, or friend.

Does it matter what type of potty-chair I use?

That really depends on you and your child's preference. Some parents like a removable bowl or cup (to dump the urine or BM), other parents do not. Buy whatever safety approved potty-chair that you like. Just be sure that your child uses the potty-chair rather than a seat adapter for the potty party because there are times when you will need to sit on the toilet while she is sitting on her potty.

What if my child rarely urinates?

He is most likely not drinking enough liquid. Aim for a cup of liquid an hour (minimum during the potty party). You might also want to visit your pediatrician for some suggestions.

Can my child watch his favorite television shows during the potty party?

Absolutely not. You can watch potty-training videos when you're working with the doll or during lunch. But in the afternoon, when you're potty training your child, you really need to stick with books or theme activities and keep your conversation focused on the topic of potty training.

Who potty trains the doll, me or my child?

It's a combination of both. You are basically guiding your child to teach the doll and giving him all the credit for doing it well. If you have a doll that wets on command, then you will be guiding your child until he gets the hang of making the doll wet. If you do not have a doll that wets on command or you are using a stuffed animal, then you need to distract your child by suggesting he go get the wipes or toilet paper (preferably from across the bathroom) while you secretly squirt the liquid into the potty to simulate the doll or animal going potty. (Be sure that your child does not see you squirt the liquid into the potty; hide the liquid container behind the doll's back.)

Who is responsible for emptying the potty bowl or cup and flushing the toilet?

Think of you and your child as a team. Take turns and make it fun. Congratulate him for being so careful. If he accidentally drops or spills the bowl or cup, just say calmly, "Accidents happen. Let's clean this up together." (If you have carpeting in the bathroom, the theme floor cloths work very well for spill protection.)

Can I check my e-mail or talk on the telephone during the potty party?

No! Especially not in the afternoon when you are working directly with your child. If you do anything that takes your focus away from your child, accidents are likely to happen. Put an automatic vacation response on your e-mail. Let your answering machine take your calls or tell people you'll call them back. You might even record an outgoing message announcing that you and your child are having a potty party and encourage callers to leave a message congratulating your child for being a big kid. You can play the messages at the Grand Finale Big Kid Celebration at the end of the day. If there are calls or e-mails you must handle, take care of them while your child takes her nap.

What type of big boy/big girl underpants work best for a child?

I suggest buying a size larger than your child would normally wear. Make sure the waistband is loose enough that your child can pull the pants down quickly. Look for big-kid underpants that fit the party theme. Dress the doll in them in the morning and give your child his own wrapped up in the afternoon to make them even more exciting for your child.

How often do I inspect my child's underwear to make sure it is still dry during the second part of training?

Approximately every five to ten minutes. You want to say something like, "Wow honey, looks like you're a big boy now. Your pants are all dry." Guide his hand with yours when you say this to help him feel his dry underwear.

How can I be sure my child really understands the difference between wet and dry?

Guide her to touch the doll's underwear when it is *dry* and *wet* during training—especially when it's wet. You use this same procedure during the afternoon portion of the party when you are working with your child. After he puts on his big boy pants, immediately guide his hand with yours to his underwear and say something like, "Great job honey! I knew you could have dry underpants too. Feel how dry they are, Yay!!" Give him a high-five and big hug.

What can I do to guarantee my child will urinate during the potty party?

Offer a variety of beverages. If one beverage doesn't work, offer something else. Have Sipping Races with your child and use fun cups and crazy straws. Remember it's important for *you* to drink a lot too. Shoot for two cups of liquid per hour. The more you drink, the greater opportunity for your child to see you urinate on the toilet. The minimum amount of liquid your child should consume during a potty party is *one cup every hour.*

What if my child still won't drink a lot of liquids?

Offer treats that will make your child *want* to drink. A Saltine cracker with a dab of peanut butter, one or two miniature rice cakes, a small pretzel, or a couple chips are examples of treats that will make your child thirsty. Also, encourage your child to drink by holding the cup up to his mouth and saying something like "Take just three more sips for Mommy and I'll take three sips too." If he drinks the extra sips, give him a high-five and praise him.

What if my child starts talking about topics unrelated to the potty party?

Then your child is a normal toddler. Seriously, kids at this age are going to bring up all sorts of topics that have nothing to do with potty training. This is a chance for you to really listen to what your child thinks about and cares about. You can even ask questions like, "What is it about that story that makes you the happiest?" or "What would you have done if you were the kid in the book?" Once you understand what your child is communicating, link his thought back to the topic of toilet training. For instance, if he says the part of the story that made him the happiest was that the bear won the race, you might say something like, "It's fun to do our best, isn't it! I bet Dolly is having fun because she is doing her best at being a big girl, isn't she?" Use this technique throughout the party to continually bring the focus back to the most exciting topic of all—potty training!

What should I do if my child does not follow a command or an instruction that I give him?

Just begin to do the action and involve her in whatever you're doing. If you say, "Let's help Dolly pull her underpants down," and your child doesn't respond, gently guide her hands to pull down the doll's pants while saying, "Here honey, why don't we do this together. When you help me, it's a lot easier! Thank you, and Dolly thanks you too."

What if my child is easily distracted or not paying attention to something I ask her to do?

Gently touch her on the shoulder so she looks at you before and while you are giving instructions. Then repeat what she may not have heard.

How should I respond if I ask my child a prompting question about using the potty and he answers incorrectly?

If you say, "What do we do when we have an accident and we have to practice?" and your child says something other than "We sit on the potty," say something like "That's one answer, isn't it?" And then continue by saying, "And when we have an accident we sit on the potty to practice because everyone needs to practice, and it helps build our potty-training memory muscles too." The key is to give your child the correct answer without correcting her or making her feel bad for giving an answer other than the one you were looking for.

My child doesn't speak very well. Will a potty party still work?

As long as you and your child have established an effective way of communicating, you should be able to understand each other during potty training. Just keep your verbal instructions simple and be very clear about what you want the doll and your child to do. Most children, regardless of their language skill level, respond more dramatically to an adult's actions and attitude than to anything the person says.

What should the doll be wearing during the potty party?

Her big-kid theme underpants or plain cloth underpants.

How important is it for the doll to have accidents?

Extremely important. It is imperative to the entire learning process; learning through imitation and learning through teaching. Let your child *discover* the doll's wet underpants and BMs. Together, you and your child should say to the doll, "Dolly, we do not have accidents in our underpants." You then want your child to tell the doll she needs to practice sitting on the potty. Explain to your child that the reason Dolly needs practice after each accident is so next time she'll remember not to go in her underpants.

What if my child won't sit long enough on the potty to actually urinate?

One of the secrets to getting your child to sit long enough is to pull down your pants and sit on the toilet while he sits on the potty-chair. You can also engage his mind so he is entertained while on the potty. This will help him relax and sit long enough to go. Use flash cards with animals or letters on them. You might blow bubbles so he can swat at them, play a game of I Spy with my little eye, or read the potty books you put in the bathroom. Be creative and keep it fun. Books that require interactivity, such as the *I Spy, BrainQuest,* and Lift-the-Flap series of books are good choices. If neither of you urinate after a few minutes, pull up your pants and leave the bathroom.

How long do I continue using the doll?

The doll is the focal point of the first half of training and remains the focal point until your child has made the connection that urine and BMs go in the toilet. During the second half of the party, the doll assumes more of a supporting role, taking a backseat position. The doll is still visible and included, but the focus is now on you guiding your child, rather than the child directing the doll.

During the second half of the party, how can I find out if my child needs to use the potty without directly asking him "Do you have to use the potty?"

Watch for signs that he has to urinate, such as fidgeting, jumping around, or holding his genitals. When you see these signs, don't ask; *tell* your child it's time to go potty. Make it a game and challenge him: "Let's see who can get there first." Remember to use the suggestion/command technique explained in chapter five.

If your child isn't demonstrating any of the classic "I have to pee" signs but he's had a lot of liquids and it's been about fifteen to twenty minutes since the last bathroom visit, then I suggest you hop, skip, or have a leap frog race into the bathroom.

If you're one of the lucky parents whose children actually understand the question, "Do you have to use the potty?" and respond accurately, congratulations. If you're like the rest of us, then you'll need to guide your child by saying things like, "Honey, show me and Dolly how we walk into the bathroom and go pee-pee. You are such a great teacher!"

What if my child is fidgeting as if she has to go, but not saying anything about using the potty?

You will want to make a comment about the function of the potty and/or use some of the comments in the Phrases That Pay dialogue in chapter six.

What should I do or say if my child hops off the potty?

Shriek at the top of your lungs as if he just shattered a $5,000 vase. Okay, obviously that's not the right thing to do, but plenty of parents overreact like this, or close enough to scare the pee out of their kids. I suggest a calmer approach. If he's been seated for a few minutes, he may simply not need to go. Don't push the issue. Instead, congratulate him for being such a big boy for sitting on the potty. If he starts fidgeting or you see full bladder signs after you get back to the party room, say something like "Guess what, honey, I didn't think I had to use the potty a few minutes ago, but now I feel like I need to go pee-pee. Read me a book on your potty while I sit and go pee-pee on mine." Don't hang around for your child to say no, just dash off to the bathroom with a "I'll beat you there."

After I model urinating in the toilet, should I pick out a sticker and put it on my child's Potty Progress Chart?

Absolutely! If you act like you are very proud of yourself for being a big kid, your child will follow your lead and attempt to be a big kid too—just like you.

Should we pick out stickers and put them on the chart even when we do not actually urinate or have a BM?

Without a doubt. Sitting and trying is something to be congratulated for too.

What if my child really isn't into stickers?

A lot of children really love to rubber stamp things, and some like the press-on tattoos. Rubber stamps and temporary tattoos are available everywhere these days and they come in a variety of shapes and designs. You won't have any problem matching your stamp to your theme, especially if you go to a rubber stamp store. Most of the ink pads are nontoxic, but it never hurts to read the packaging. Kids love to stamp or tattoo the back of their hands, arms, and legs too. Why not join in the fun and give yourself a stamp too?

Should my little boy stand or sit on the potty?

During the potty party, you will definitely want him to sit. It is easier to play games and you might get lucky and he'll have a BM when he urinates. Don't worry. All little boys learn to urinate while standing when they go to preschool or see other little boys or their dads doing it.

What types of positive reinforcement should I use to motivate my child?

Plenty of verbal praise, physical praise (hugs, pats, high-five hand slaps, kisses on the cheek, little dances of joy around the room), tasty bite-size treats, small, playful treats, a lot of yummy beverages, a phone call, card, or letter from someone congratulating his success. Or have your child call Grandma or Grandpa to share the good news.

Should I use this reinforcement during the entire potty party?

Yes, congratulate all his successes.

How do I respond when my child has an accident?

Do not scold, yell at, spank, or hit your child. Tell her, "Accidents happen when we are first learning something new." Then encourage her to clean up the mess and change her wet or dirty clothes. After accidents, have her practice walking to the potty and sitting down for a few minutes. This helps her build her memory muscles and helps reinforce the idea of getting to the potty in time. Most kids do not find a lot of joy in potty practice. So if you feel your child is resistant, you might want to include yourself in the practice. Say something like "I'll practice with you because it helps me remember when I need to go potty too." Then have a bit of dialogue about the importance of getting to the bathroom in time.

Is it okay for a child to wear pants or a jumper?

No. For the first half of the party, she should wear a diaper or pull-ups. During the second half of the party, your child should be wearing her big-kid theme underpants.

What type of shirt is best to wear during the potty party?

An undershirt. They are generally shorter than T-shirts, which usually hang down too low and inhibit the child from quickly pulling down his underwear.

What if my child isn't interested in participating in a potty party?

Don't worry. In the hundreds of parents I've worked with, there has yet to be a child who doesn't get excited when they get the doll for a present and then happily join in the fun of a potty party.

What should I do if my child refuses to follow directions?

If you followed all the instructions in the earlier part of the book and have enthusiastically encouraged your child to potty train the doll, and you still are meeting with resistance, it might be that your child just isn't ready to be potty trained. Go back and review the readiness signs in chapter two. If your child isn't ready, wait a few months and try again. If your child *is* ready, consider bringing in a Potty Party Pinch Hitter.

If my child isn't completely potty trained by the end of the potty party, should she go back into diapers?

No. Hopefully during the party you made it clear that "diapers are for little babies." You will want to dress her in her big-kid underpants the morning after the party and start where you left off. See chapter seven for reinforcing potty-training suggestions.

In the first few weeks following the potty party, how should I handle accidents, nighttime protection, treats and positive reinforcement, and outer clothing?

For accidents, always reassure her that accidents happen. Help her clean up the mess and encourage her to change her own clothes. You'll want to tell her that she needs to keep building her potty training memory muscles by walking to the potty and sitting for a couple of minutes.

Your child should continue to wear his pull-ups at night until he has several dry nights or weeks in a row. No diapers. Remember and reinforce that diapers are for babies.

Eventually you'll want to phase out the treats, but there is little harm in a few M&Ms or their carob cousins for the first few days after the potty party. Send a few treat cups with him to preschool. They won't mind helping him reinforce his new skill. You'll also want to continue to verbally praise him and give him hugs and other physical praise for a long time. You child will work extra hard to stay dry over the weeks and months if he knows how happy it makes you when he goes on the potty.

For outerwear, dress your child in pants with loose-fitting elastic waistbands, such as jogging pants (with no belt) or anything easy to remove.

8. potty progress

Children are likely to live up to what you believe of them.

—LADY BIRD JOHNSON

No matter how well your child did during his potty-training party, you will need to reinforce his new behavior until it becomes a comfortable new habit. The guidelines for potty practice are the same as they were for the potty party. Use lots of positive reinforcement, praise, and patience, and never reprimand your child for having an accident. Rather, just like during the potty party, you correct and reprimand the doll or the stuffed animal.

The day after the potty party when your child wakes up, tell her that her dolly had an accident. You might say something like, "Nancy, this morning before you woke up, Dolly went pee-pee in her big-girl pants. We don't go pee-pee in our big-girl pants, do we?" Show her the doll and let her feel the doll's wet underpants. Together with your child, correct the doll. "Dolly, no more pee-pee in your pants!"

Guide your child to work with her doll. "Why don't you take off Dolly's wet underpants and put them in the sink so we can wash them. And take Dolly into the bathroom and let her sit on the potty in case she has to go again. If she doesn't go potty, it will still help her to remember that she's a big girl and build her potty-training memory muscles."

After your child takes her doll off the potty and puts dry underpants on her, tell your child, "Now it's your turn to go on the potty. I'll race you!"

YOU CAN SAY THAT AGAIN!

"Correction does much, but encouragement does more."

—JOHANN WOLFGANG VON GOETHE

Remember that it's rarely a good idea to ask your toddler if he has to use the potty. Even if he's doing the pee-pee jig or grabbing his crotch, he'll most likely say no. So skip the question and go right for the suggestion/command. Race him to the bathroom, suggest that you skip or hop there, or simply say, "Mommy's going to sit on the big potty now and you get to sit on your potty too!"

Later in the day, put some baby food prunes in the doll's big boy underpants and guide your child to discover that the doll has made a BM in his pants. You might sniff the doll and say, "Tommy, do you smell something? I think Dolly went potty in his pants!" Let your son take the doll's underpants off and discover the prunes. Then, lead him to correct the doll. "No more poopy in your pants!" Together with your child, take the poop-filled underpants to the toilet and flush the prunes down. Then suggest that the doll sit on the potty for a while and continue to build his potty-training memory muscles.

Potty Practice on the Go

Once your child has successfully used her potty-chair or seat adapter at home, it's time to take the show on the road. Folding seat adapters are great for traveling, visiting friends and relatives, and for public restrooms. I suggest planning a Potty Parade for the day following the potty party. Talk to some nearby friends, relatives, and neighbors ahead of time. Ask if you can stop by to let your little one practice using her seat adapter or the big potty so she can get comfortable doing the deed wherever nature calls.

Once your daytime diaper graduate has used a few toilets in other people's homes, up the ante by taking him to a public restroom. Begin with a place that he loves to go, like Chuck E. Cheese, McDonald's, a nearby playground, or a store like Babies R Us or Toys R Us.

When you first arrive at a store, restaurant, museum, or playground, make it a habit to locate and stop in the restroom before you do anything else. You and your child can both try to go. If nothing happens, nothing lost. But now you know where the restroom is, and when your child needs to go it will be his second time in that restroom, which generally helps children relax a little. (Explain that a bathroom and a restroom are actually the same thing. Some kids think potty trivia, like that in England they call the entire room the toilet, is funny!)

Armed with your folding seat adapter decorated with your toddler's favorite stickers, try to make going into the new bathroom as stress-free as possible. You might distract your child by asking him to sing you his favorite song or tell you a story about one of his favorite cartoon characters. This is very important because even as adults, most of us dislike using public restrooms. Our children can easily pick up on what we're feeling, particularly when we walk in the door and immediately start issuing cautions like "Don't touch anything. These places are crawling with germs!" When we get worked up, our kids do too and then they contract their muscles and suddenly they no longer have to go. Unfortunately, the urge is sure to return as soon as they relax, which is likely to happen as soon as you're miles away from the nearest bathroom.

If you don't have a folding seat adapter or you don't have it with you, calmly help your child to use the adult toilet by holding him. Although it's a hassle, it's often worth it to take your

FROM THE MOUTHS OF BABES

My two-year-old son, Brian, recently showed an interest in using the potty. We were at Grandma's house when I noticed he was squatting and grunting in the corner. I said, "Let's go sit on Grandma's potty." Within two minutes he was screaming for everyone to come and look. "I poofed, I poofed!" Now he thinks he's a big boy and is constantly sniffing out his baby brother. We are notified when Dominic's diaper is filled with a very loud "E-U, you poofed!"

—MARY FRANCESCA HEALY

child's pants and underpants off before attempting this acrobatic feat. Lift up your child and hold her over the toilet seat, facing the back of the toilet. This gives you more room and also helps your child to focus on the task at hand, rather than what's going on outside the bathroom stall.

If it's summer or you live in a warm climate, teach your child how to go outside without a potty or a seat adapter. Lots of kids get a kick out of this, and if your family does a lot of outdoor activities, this new skill is bound to come in handy. Learning to urinate outside is typically easier for boys, since they can stand up and often enjoy peeing on a variety of objects. If your child is a girl, show her how she can pull her pants down around her ankles and then hold on to a tree or other stationary object to make squatting easier. (Lots of toddlers can easily squat without holding on to anything!)

If your family is planning a vacation that involves taking a bus, train, or airplane in the near future, it's also a good idea to prepare your child by telling him about what these types of bathrooms look like. They are very small and the toilets are really cool because they have places on the walls where people can hold on. Also describe the way it will sound in the moving bathroom. Tell him that it's really cool to hear the sound of the train clicking on the tracks or the plane flying through the air. Obviously, you'll want to present this information as a fun adventure, rather than making it sound frightening or intimidating in any way.

CELEBRITY SCOOP

"All kids need is a little help, a little hope, and somebody who believes in them."

Earvin "Magic" Johnson

When you take your child to a large place like the zoo or an amusement park, begin the outing by looking at the map and pointing out the locations of all the restrooms. Although the map probably won't make any sense to her, you can teach her what the restroom icon looks like and show her where they are on the map. Point to the restrooms, one at a time, and say, "Look, Sarah, there are four big-girl bathrooms here. There's one by the merry-go-round, one next to the hotdog stand, another one by the cotton candy stand, and one more right next to the video arcade!" Determine which two bathrooms are the closest to the park entrance and let her choose which one to visit first. Reinforce the idea that you know she's a big girl now and that she will tell you when she needs to urinate and the two of you will go to the nearest restroom.

Although the Potty Parade is designed to increase your child's comfort and reinforce his potty habit, it's still a good idea to bring his own potty-chair along for the ride. If you have a van or SUV, consider bringing the potty-chair along when you go out to do errands, especially when you know you will be away from home for more than a few hours. (Camping toilets also work great if your vehicle is large enough to accommodate one.) To make clean up easy, line the potty-chair cup with two plastic bags, one inside the other (just in case one breaks). After your little one uses the potty, all you need to do is seal or tie the bag and drop it into the next trash can you see. Always stop the car in a safe place before helping your child get out of his carseat or seat belt to use his potty-chair.

For quick trips like going to the grocery store, when you don't want to take the potty-chair with you, bring along a coffee can or plastic ice cream pail with a lid. Line the container with the stuffing from a disposable diaper to reduce splashback.

DID YOU KNOW?

Disposable diapers are a $6.5 *billion* U.S. industry.

It's also a good idea to keep a stash of disposable pull-up diapers on hand and use your better judgment for when to use them. For example, with all the walking and long lines in amusement parks, department stores, and malls, consider letting your recently toilet-trained child wear disposables as a "just in case" measure, and make sure she understands this is what's happening. Carry little facial tissue packs and a handful of individually wrapped wet wipes in case the restroom is out of toilet paper or your child needs more than a dry cleaning.

Keep the Practice Going When You Won't Be Home

Tell your child that you are going away for the day (or a few days) and let him know who will be taking care of him while you're gone. Remind him to encourage his doll or stuffed animal to keep up potty practice. Tell him that his caregiver knows all about him being a big boy and using the potty, and that she will help him just like you do.

Make sure your spouse, baby-sitter, or child-care provider

(even if it's Grandma) knows the potty protocol that you've established and that they are willing and able to pinch hit while you're gone. This includes knowing the words you use for body parts and functions and the frequency that you suggest your child be directed to the bathroom to sit on the potty.

AWARD-WINNING ADVICE

At night I stopped my children from drinking liquids about one hour before their bedtime. Then right before they fell asleep, I would put them on the potty.

—LISA MONROE

If possible, check in by phone. If your child's caregiver says he is using the potty, take a moment to praise him. If he's not, tell him that you know he's a big boy and he probably just feels a little different since you're not there. Then assure him that he will use the potty before you call back. Say something like, "I know when I call back after dinner, you will be able to tell me that you went on the potty, just like you do when I'm at home."

If, for whatever reason, your child doesn't continue her habit while you're gone, you'll need to spend a few hours reinforcing it with a mini version of the potty party when you return. There's no need to make as big a deal this time because she's already a big girl and this is just a refresher course. But treats and total attention will still be required for this follow-up session. Whatever you do, don't make your child feel bad, call her a baby, or give her any negative feedback.

Accidents Happen

When we learn something new—whether we are children or adults—making mistakes is part of the educational process. No one has ever learned to ride a bike without falling or learned to set or clear the table without dropping a dish or a glass.

Accidents are normal from time to time, especially in the weeks following the potty party. Never scold or punish your child for having an accident. Instead, assure your child that you believe in his ability to master this new skill. Tell him, "Everybody makes mistakes when we learn something new. But, we just keep practicing and pretty soon, we're really good at it. You'll see. That's exactly what will happen for you. The more you practice the better you'll get."

Establish a No Tolerance for Teasing rule with all of your family members, especially older brothers and sisters who may not realize how damaging their teasing is to their younger sibling. Make it clear that no teasing or taunting of any kind will be tolerated. Decide ahead of time what the consequence

POTTY-TRAINING BOOT CAMP TIP

For the first few weeks after my daughter was potty trained, she occasionally had accidents and wet her pants. Helping her to change her clothes and wash her pants was no problem, but I have to admit I was worried about the damage that urine could do to our new furniture. I bought a blanket that was made for incontinent dogs and told Heather this was her special big-girl blanket. It was soft fleece on the side she sat on and waterproof on the other side. As it turned out, she only had one accident while sitting on it, but the peace of mind was worth the money and the effort!

for breaking the rule is, and clearly communicate that to your children. Reward your children for praising and supporting their younger sibling with potty practice. You can even give them special badges that identify them as Official Potty Promoters that you made or bought ahead of time.

Meanwhile, although accidents are par for the learning course, if your child is having one or more accidents every day or every couple of days, there might be more going on than meets the eye–or the nose. If your child isn't able to stay dry for two hours or has frequent accidents when there's a bathroom nearby, make an appointment with his pediatrician, just to make sure that everything is physically okay. Some of the reasons for incontinence include allergic reactions to certain foods or drinks, side effects of some medications, and even undiagnosed illnesses.

Keep in mind that when children are sick, accidents are common until they feel better and are once again able to control their bladder and bowels. Increase your child's comfort and ease her stress by suggesting she wear her "just in case" disposables until she feels better.

TAMING THE POTTY BULLY

"Children today are tyrants. They contradict their parents, gobble their food, and tyrannize their teachers."

—Socrates

Very few children will use the threat of wetting or soiling their pants to manipulate their parents or caregivers, but some will.

The secret here is to unequivocally refuse to give in to any threats that your child issues. If he goes into "Toilet Tyrant" mode, in a very calm voice, simply state, "You know you're a big boy now and that you can use the potty. So, since you're a big boy, if you go in your pants, you will have to wash your clothes and clean the floor where it gets wet. That will mean extra work for both of us and it won't make either of us happy."

If your little angel carries out the threat, complete whatever you were doing (if at all possible) before helping him to remove his wet or soiled clothes or cleaning him up. If you drop everything and give him your immediate attention, he will feel that his threats were successful and may repeat the act again and again. Establish a clear policy: "In this family, we don't negotiate when people make threats!"

Reversing a Backslide

If your child has a series of accidents and her pediatrician determines that she is in good health, there might be something going on emotionally. Oftentimes, if a child's stress level goes up, her potty prowess goes down.

These are events that can increase stress and trigger backsliding:

- Starting a new daycare or preschool
- Being separated from a parent
- Experiencing the death of a family member or pet
- Moving to a new home
- Acquiring a new baby brother or sister
- Witnessing an increase in parental arguments

To reverse backsliding, give your child some time in disposable pull-ups while she emotionally adjusts to the change. Be clear that this is a temporary measure, and empathize with her by saying, "When we go through a difficult time, it can be hard to remember to use the potty. For now, wear your pull-up disposable pants just in case. In a few weeks, you'll feel better and be ready to use the potty again." When a few weeks have passed, have a mini–potty party (just a few hours) with the doll to refresh your child's habit.

Bedwetting

As I discussed earlier, children learn to stay dry during the day before they learn to stay dry while napping or during the night. Most children who wet their beds while they are sleeping do so because they do not respond to the internal signal of a full bladder. I strongly suggest that you put disposable pull-up diapers

EXPERT CONTRIBUTION

Nutrition Can Reduce Your Toddler's Constipation
Contributed by Cinda Chima, M.S., R.D.,
Assistant Professor, Nutrition and Dietetics,
The University of Akron, Ohio

Parents often have questions about the relationship
between toilet teaching, bowel function, and diet.
After all, what goes in affects what comes out.

CONSTIPATION

About 3 percent of pediatric office visits and 25 percent of pediatric gastroenterologist visits are related
to what is charmingly called a "defecation disorder."
Some of these are false alarms. For instance, a parent may expect her child to have a bowel movement
every day. But normal bowel frequency can vary
from several times a day to several times a week
(average 1.4 per day). This is quite a range!

Signs of constipation include infrequent stools
that are hard or difficult to pass, painful BMs, and
runny stool. Painful BMs can cause a child to hold
stool or to be afraid to have a BM in the toilet.
Contact your doctor if you think your child is
constipated.

Once the immediate problem is resolved, take
steps to prevent a recurrence. Establishing healthy
bowel habits is key. Tell your child not to wait if he
needs to have a BM. Have your child use the
bathroom about the same time every day (after
meals is a good time). Children who are physically
active tend to have less trouble with constipation.
Ask your doctor about any medication your child is
taking, because some medicine affects bowel
habits. Improving your child's diet should make
constipation less likely in the future.

Tips to Prevent Constipation

◆ Increase fiber in your child's diet. Children who
  have a high amount of fiber in their diets are
  less likely to be constipated.

◆ Encourage your child to eat more fruits, vegetables, bran, and fiber. Offer fruits and vegetables
  with every meal and for snacks. A good target
  is five servings of fruits and vegetables a day.
  Peas and beans are especially good sources of
  fiber.

◆ Choose whole grain cereals like shredded wheat,
  oatmeal, and raisin bran.

◆ Select whole grain breads, muffins, and granola
  bars. The first ingredient on the label should be
  whole wheat flour or some other "whole" grain.
  "Wheat flour" is not enough. Bread should have
  at least 3 grams of fiber per serving. Breads
  with dried fruits deliver even more fiber.

◆ Be sure your child drinks plenty of fluids.

DIARRHEA

Diarrhea is a sudden increase in the frequency and
looseness of bowel movements. One loose stool
does not mean diarrhea; it probably just means the
child ate something unusual. Most diarrhea in toddlers is caused by mild gastrointestinal infections.
Other causes include food poisoning or food intoler-
ances. Antibiotics are also a common cause of diarrhea in children. Contact your doctor for advice if
your child develops diarrhea.

Diet Causes of Diarrhea

◆ Diarrhea in young children is often caused by
  too much juice or sweetened beverages. Some
  juices such as pear and apple contain sorbitol, a
  sugar alcohol that is poorly digested. Sorbitol

does not appear on the label because it is naturally found in fruit. Think your child never drinks pear juice? It is commonly used in juice drink mixtures, including some of the "100 percent juice" beverages.

- Many liquid medications are made with sorbitol and other sugar-free sweeteners, which can sometimes cause diarrhea.

- If your child has persistent diarrhea (more than two weeks) and other causes have been ruled out, your pediatrician may diagnose toddler's diarrhea. If your child has toddler's diarrhea, it may be helpful to cut back on juice and other sweet beverages and add fiber and fat to the diet.

Treatment of Acute Diarrhea

- If your child is dehydrated, your pediatrician may recommend an oral rehydration therapy formula such as Pedialyte or Infalyte.

- While some doctors still favor the classic BRAT diet (bananas, rice, applesauce, and dry toast) to treat diarrhea, the American Academy of Pediatrics disagrees. According to the Academy, the BRAT diet is low in energy, protein, and fat. While the BRAT diet is usually well tolerated, there is no evidence it is helpful.

- The Academy recommends an unrestricted, age-appropriate diet in children with diarrhea. Studies show that unrestricted diets do not worsen the course or symptoms of mild diarrhea and can actually decrease stool output. The Academy recommends complex carbohydrates (rice, wheat, potatoes, bread, and cereals), lean meats, yogurt, fruits, and vegetables. Most children (80 percent) will tolerate milk, though some may experience a temporary intolerance to dairy products. Yogurt might be worth a try, since there is some evidence it can replenish beneficial intestinal bacteria and restore bowel health.

Myths About Diet and Diarrhea

- The "clear liquid" diet (juice, soda, sweetened gelatin) that is often first offered to sick children is a bad idea. Foods high in sugar (including tea, juices, and soft drinks) can make diarrhea worse.

- Bowel rest is equally bad for most children with diarrhea. Children who are fed through episodes of diarrhea tend to recover faster.

on your child for naps and nighttime sleeping for the first few weeks or even months after she is potty trained.

Make it a habit to sit on the potty as soon as your child wakes up from a nap and first thing every morning. When your child stays dry for several naps in a row, allow him to nap with his big-boy pants. When he stays dry at night for a week or more, allow him to sleep without a diaper and see what happens. If your child has an accident while sleeping, remember that it's not his fault. Simply help him get cleaned up and tell him there's no reason to feel badly or ashamed because everyone

TIPS FOR INCREASING FIBER IN YOUR CHILD'S DIET

★ Note: Food choices should be age-appropriate in size and texture. ★

FOOD	GROUP USE
CEREALS	Whole grain cereals like oatmeal, shredded wheat, raisin bran, granolas. The first ingredient on the label should be a whole grain. Choose cereals with at least 2 grams of fiber per serving. Mix a high-fiber cereal with one your child likes.
BREAD	Choose breads made from whole grain flours, such as whole grain muffins, bran muffins, whole grain bagels, and English muffins. The first ingredient on the label should say whole wheat flour. Choose breads with at least 3 grams of fiber per serving. Some breads have added fiber in the form of wheat bran and oatmeal.
GRAINS	Whole wheat pasta, brown rice, barley, wild rice, and rice and pasta with beans are all good choices.
FRUITS AND VEGETABLES	All fruits and vegetables contain fiber. Corn, peas, beans, broccoli, cauliflower, raspberries, strawberries, blueberries, blackberries, and figs are especially good sources. Choose fruits and vegetables that are age-appropriate. Eat fruits with skins.
MEAL TIME	
BREAKFAST	Instant oatmeal with raisins, milk, whole wheat muffin, orange juice
LUNCH	Chicken barley soup with vegetables, fresh apple slices, milk
DINNER	Roast pork, mashed sweet potatoes, broccoli, whole grain roll, milk
SNACKS	Fresh fruit, preferably with the skin, cut to suitable size. Graham crackers and oatmeal cookies or bars. After age three, popcorn, nuts and seeds, granola bars.

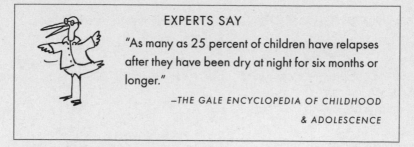

EXPERTS SAY

"As many as 25 percent of children have relapses after they have been dry at night for six months or longer."

—THE GALE ENCYCLOPEDIA OF CHILDHOOD
& ADOLESCENCE

has accidents until their body learns to wake them up to go to the potty.

If bedwetting continues after a child has had daytime bladder control for several months, explore this issue with your pediatrician, just to make sure that your child is healthy and does not have a hidden or undiagnosed condition.

EXPERTS SAY

"There are more than 5 million children in the United States who wet the bed. To give parents a sense of how big 5 million really is, Dr. Bennett says if you invited 5 million children to see a professional baseball game, you would need a hundred stadiums to find them all a seat."

—DR. HOWARD BENNETT, WAKING UP DRY

Let the Fun and Games Begin!

If you want your child to enjoy learning, develop self-confidence, and believe in his own abilities, set the stage for the rest of his life by making potty training a positive process.

Children who receive sincere praise and acknowledgment from their parents, siblings, and other adults tend to learn faster and enjoy the process much more. When a child learns while having fun, her self-esteem goes up and she develops a

EXPERT CONTRIBUTION

Secrets for Super Poop-ers and Pee-ers
Contributed by Timothy P. Culbert, M.D.,
Medical Director, Integrative Medicine and Cultural
Care, Children's Hospitals and Clinics,
Minneapolis/St. Paul, Minnesota

WHAT YOU CAN DO ABOUT CONSTIPATION

Beyond dietary intervention, parents can:

* Encourage physical activity.

* Address defecation anxiety with reassurance about soft, comfortable "happy poops" that will develop with regular BMs. Teach kids basic relaxation techniques. Work with a child psychologist or developmental pediatrician if anxiety is severe.

* Put the child on a stool softener/laxative such as senna, benefiber, or glucomannan, which are over the counter, or a prescription medicine such as MiraLax or lactulose.

* Use lots of social praise and behavioral rewards for good cooperation and effort.

* Be patient and look for small steps in the right direction. Don't expect immediate regular stools in the toilet right away.

* As a way to keep them more focused on the process, continue your child's sticker chart to track daily practice, clean underwear, pooping, peeing, and related activities for several weeks.

TIPS FOR SHAPING TOILETING BEHAVIOR

If your child is hiding and/or withholding stool, the first step is to reward him or her for producing stool in the diaper or pull-up each day. If he has some defecation anxiety and is fearful of painful BMs, it can be useful to teach basic relaxation before and during defecation. Slow "belly breathing" is a good technique for kids: Have him breathe in through his nose to the count of two and then out through his mouth to the count of four. This can be facilitated with the use of bubbles and pinwheels, which have the added benefit of being good distractions.

Another technique that kids like is progressive muscle relaxation. This involves alternately squeezing and then relaxing different muscle groups throughout the body in cycles of ten seconds. For example, you can have your child contract then relax her feet, legs, stomach, arms, shoulders, and face muscles as different groups. Using a stool softener is also helpful. Reassuring her that the more she poops the more her poop will be "happy poops" is a nice way to frame it with language.

YOU CAN SAY THAT AGAIN!

"Great works are performed, not by strength, but by perseverance."

—SAMUEL JOHNSON

DID YOU KNOW?

Twenty percent of children are still bedwetting up to age five. Most doctors do not consider nighttime bed wetting a problem until a child is five or six years old.

strong sense of "I can do it!" Since using the potty is one of the first major skills that a child attempts to acquire, the way she feels about learning and mastering new skills is greatly influenced by how you behave while you're teaching and coaching her to use the potty.

As with all skills and habits that you teach your child, your patient persistence will make all the difference. Remember that toddlers truly want to please their parents—even in the midst of the terrible twos! They may behave as if pleasing you is the last thing they care about, but this is just a toddler's way of beginning to assert her independence.

I encourage you to take advantage of the potty party day as a way of not only teaching your child an important and necessary skill, but also as a day of bonding. The more fun you have during the party, the more fun your child will have and the more effective and enjoyable the experience will be for both of you. You will also have the deep sense of satisfaction that comes from knowing that you are giving your child your absolute best—not in the form of the presents and prizes, but with your undivided attention and unconditional love.

Party on!

resources

General Resources for Parents

American Academy of Pediatrics
P.O. Box 927
Elk Grove Village, Illinois 60009
800-433-9016
847-228-5005
www.aap.org

Zero to Three
2000 M Street NW, Suite 200
Washington, D.C. 20036
www.zerotothree.org

NATIONAL ENURESIS SOCIETY (NES)

This association was formed to advise parents and professionals of methods to help children overcome bed-wetting, rather than just waiting until it is outgrown. NES is part of the National Kidney Foundation. For information, contact: NES, 1-800-622-9010, or visit www.kidney.org

THE NATIONAL ASSOCIATION FOR CONTINENCE

This is a nonprofit organization whose mission is to educate anyone (regardless of age) about the causes and cures for incontinence. Call 800-252-3337 for a free packet of information entitled "Seeking Treatment." Or visit their website, www.nafc.org

Potty-Training Supplies

DOLLS THAT WET

Dolls that wet and are ready for toilet training all vary greatly in terms of price: Emma and Paul from Corolle; Aquini Drink and Wet Doll; Baby Born Doll by Baby Born; Little Mommy's Helper from Mattel; Baby Alive from Kenner; Betsy Wetsy, Tiny Tears, and Magic Potty Baby from Tyco Toys; Potty Time Tinkles from Goldberger; www.pottytrainingconcepts.com has potty training dolls too.

WATERPROOF BLANKET

Waterproof blankets are perfect long after the potty party is over. Many boot camp moms use them, not only for play and picnicking outside on the lawn and days at the beach, but also as easy clean-up drop cloths indoors. Whatever the mess or spill, pop the whole blanket right into the washer and dryer. Many companies carry them: outlets like Orvis often sell them as waterproof picnic blankets. Camping stores and catalogues like REI or Gander Mountain market them as waterproof outdoor blankets. A lot of stores that carry baby products, like BABIES R US, also carry baby blankets with a rubberized backing on one side.

CLOTH TRAINING PANTS

Options in cloth training pants are numerous in both design and style. You will probably need (I know I did) cloth underpants that offer extra absorbency in the crotch. You never know where you'll be when your child needs it (or how far away from a toilet).

If your child has difficulty pulling up cloth training pants, many boot camp moms had a lot of success using a cloth training wrap with Velcro closing tabs. Cloth training wraps are absorbent and machine washable. A lot of brands also include a waterproof outer layer.

Brand names for daytime or nighttime cloth training pants include Bummis, Bumkins, Dappi, Gerber, Kushies/Kooshies, and Nikky. These brands are available in most stores and baby mail-order catalogues.

Some catalogues and Internet sites offer exclusive-to-them cloth diaper and training pants:

One Step Ahead   800-274-8440; www.onestepahead.com

Perfectly Safe   800-837-5437; www.perfectlysafe.com

The Right Start   800-548-8531; www.rightstart.com

These home-based businesses also offer catalogues:

www.babybunz.com   800-676-4559

www.katieskisses.com   888-881-0404

www.thebabylane.com   888-387-0019

Books

CHILD DEVELOPMENT AND BEHAVIOR BOOKS FOR PARENTS

Magic Trees of the Mind: How to Nurture Your Child's Intelligence, Creativity, and Healthy Emotions from Birth Through Adolescence by Marian Diamond, Ph.D., and Janet Hopson (Penguin Group USA, 1999).

Raising Preschoolers: Parenting for Today by Dr. Sylvia Rimm, Ph.D. (Three Rivers Press, 1997).

* For a free newsletter about discipline, raising preschoolers, and principles of parenting, send a large self-addressed, stamped envelope to Dr. Sylvia Rimm, P.O. Box 32, Watertown, WI 53094, or visit www.sylviarimm.com.

Steps to Independence: Teaching Everyday Skills to Children with Special Needs, by Bruce L. Baker and Alan J. Brightman (Paul H. Brookes Publishing, 2004).

* Purchasers of this book can download all of the forms found in the book free of charge from the Brookes Publishing website. These forms are available at www.brookespublishing.com/steps.

The Five Love Languages of Children, by Gary Chapman and Ross Campbell, M.D. (Northfield Publishing, 1997).

The Secret Lives of Toddlers: A Parent's Guide to the Wonderful, Terrible, Fascinating Behavior of Children Ages 1 to 3, by Jana Murphy (Perigee, 2004).

BOOKS TO READ WHILE SITTING ON THE POTTY

There are many (as you will soon find out) potty books for children, and each book has a slightly different emphasis. I mentioned a few of my favorites earlier, but also check out book stores, visit a few different libraries to borrow a variety (library loans and rentals are the most economical way to go), or search online for titles such as the following:

Annie's Potty by Judith Caseley (Greenwillow)

Bye-Bye, Diapers by Tom Cooke (Golden Books)

Caillou-Potty Time by Joceline Sansehagrin (Chouette Editions)

Everyone Poops by Taro Gomi (Kane/Miller)

Flush the Potty by Ken Wilson-Max (Scholastic)

Going to the Potty by Fred Rogers (Putnam/Paper Star)

I Want My Potty by Tony Ross (Kane/Miller)

I Have to Go! by Robert Munsch (Annick Press)

I Have to Go by Anna Ross (Sesame Street Toddler Books)

I'm a Potty Champion! by Kitty Higgins (Barrons)

KoKo Bear's New Potty by Vicki Lansky (Book Peddlers)

Max's Potty (DK Publishing)

My Big Boy (Big Girl) Potty by Joanna Cole (Harper-Collins)

My Potty Chair by Ruth Young (Viking Kestrel)

No More Diapers by Emma Thompson (Sesame Street Picturebook Paperback)

On Your Potty by Virginia Miller (Greenwillow)

Potty Time by Guido Van Genechten (Little Simon)

Sam's Potty by Barbro Lindgren (Morrow)

The Gas We Pass by Shinta Cho (Kane/Miller)

The Potty Chronicles by Anne Reiner (Magination Press)

The Potty Book for Girls (for Boys) by A. Capucilli (Barrons)

The Princess and the Potty by Wendy Lewison (Aladdin)

The Toddler's Potty Book by Alida Allison (Dimensions)

Toilet Book by Jan Pienkowski (Dimensions)

Toilet Tales by Andrea W. Von Konigslow (Annick Press)

What to Expect When You Use the Potty by Heidi Murkoff (HarperCollins Juvenile)

What Do You Do with a Potty? by Marianne Borgardt (Dimensions)

Uh Oh! Gotta Go! by Bob McGrath (Barron's)

When You've Got to Go (Bear in the Big Blue House) by Mitchell Kriegman (Simon Spotlight)

Your New Potty by Joanna Cole (HarperCollins)

You could photocopy this list and take it to your library to check their books out, or do some interbranch loans for books and videos.

BOOKS ABOUT BED-WETTING

Waking Up Dry by Howard J. Bennett, M.D., F.A.A.P. (American Academy of Pediatrics, 2005)

Waking Up Dry: How to End Bedwetting Forever by Martin Scharf (Writer's Digest, 1986)

No More Bed-Wetting: How to Help Your Child Stay Dry by Samuel J. Arnold, M.D., F.A.C.S. (John Wiley, 1997)

Getting to Dry by Max Maizels, M.D., Diane Rosenbaum, Ph.D., and Barbara Keating, R.N., M.S. (Harvard Common Press, 1999)

BOOKS WRITTEN FOR CHILDREN WHO NEED EXTRA INSPIRATION AND SUPPORT TO OVERCOME BED-WETTING:

Accidental Lily by Sally Warner (Knopf, 2000)

Do Little Mermaids Wet Their Beds? by Jeanne Willis (Albert Whitman, 2001)

Dry All Night: The Picture Book Technique That Stops Bedwetting by Alison Mack (Little, Brown)

Dry Days, Wet Nights by Maribeth Boelts (Albert Whitman, 1996)

Sammy the Elephant & Mr. Camel: A Story to Help Children Overcome Bedwetting by Joyce C. Mills, Ph.D., and Richard J. Crowley, Ph.D. (Magination Press)

BOOKS ABOUT BELATED BOWELS

Clouds & Clocks: A Story for Children Who Soil by Matthew Galvin, M.D. (Magination Press, 800-374-2721, or visit apa.org/books)

A companion children's book to the *Sammy the Elephant* workbook above.

www.pottymd.com

This website offers numerous options for children with bedwetting or belated bowels.

Videos

POTTY VIDEOS

Most libraries have a pretty good assortment of potty-training videos, especially older videos, which still have great content but are no longer available for purchase in retail stores. Or go to Amazon.com and look under the video or baby section. Also try department stores like Toys R Us or Babies R Us, K Mart or Walmart. Here are a few titles to get you started:

I Gotta Go! (Vickilew Productions, 2004)

Comes with a bonus CD-rom so you can take the fun on the road.

Available in some stores and libraries. Or visit www.vicki lew.com

It's Potty Time (Learning Through Entertainment, 1990)

Endorsed by Duke University Medical Center. This video uses songs and a story about a birthday party to teach the steps involved in potty training and washing up. The video is also available in a hardcover book with a companion teddy bear. Call 800-237-6889 or visit www.lteinc.com

Let's Go Potty (Tapeworm, 1997)

Adorable live action video.

Potty Power (Thinkeroo, 2005)

Performed by both adults and children to interactive games and tasks with the goal of keeping the children seated long enough to go. Available in most stores and libraries.

The Potty Project (Penton Overseas, 2000)

This video was developed by a pediatrician, and it does a nice job of encouraging very young children to learn the basics of potty training.

Bear in the Big Blue House—Potty Time with Bear (Columbia Tristar, 1997)

Most kids' all-time favorite. Cute tunes, too.

Winston's Potty Chair (Parade Video, 1998)

This cartoon video was produced in cooperation with the American Medical Association.

Once Upon a Potty for Him, or ***Once Upon a Potty for Her*** (Barron's Educational, 1990)

If you like the books by the same title, then you'll love the animated and expanded video version by Alona Frankel. Available in most stores, or call 1-800-645-3476.

Parties in Cyberspace

These websites offer numerous options for parents looking for party ideas, advice, supplies, and inspiration.

www.boardmanweb.com basic party themes

www.personalizedpartyfavors.com cool ideas for your mystery potty party prize box

www.familyfun.com ideas inspired by Disney

www.pbskids.com lots of fun and games

www.fisherprice.com birthday planner type website

www.partypro.com theme ideas and supplies

www.nickjr.com even more party ideas

Birthday Express, www.birthdayexpress.com

This site offers every imaginable character party supply and helps you put your party package together. Boot camp moms really love this site, especially for the variety of theme ideas and the one stop packages, which include everything you'll need to pull your theme together. The site does a great job offering party planning advice and ideas, plus it has a feedback section to share suggestions with other parents. Keep the decorations from the potty party and incorporate them into a future birthday party.

Birthday Party Ideas, www.birthdaypartyideas.com

You'll find hundreds of cool ideas submitted by other parents like dance star, train, fishing, and princess parties. What's really great about this site is that all the tips and suggestions are described in detail and ideas are added daily. Check out some of the winning ideas and see which ones you want to use for

your child's party. All the parties come with an age recommendation, so stay away from the party ideas for older kids and
focus on the toddler selection for your potty party inspiration.

Looking for sites with games and activities for your Potty
Party? Surf here:

www.dltk-kids.com

www.gameskidsplay.com

www.family.com

www.preschooleducation.com

www.perpetualpreschool.com

www.birthdayinabox.com

www.bhg.com (Better Homes and Gardens party games)

www.amazingmoms.com

www.partygamecentral.com

Or type "party games" or "party activities" into your favorite
search engine and discover more on your own.

Where to Buy Potty Party Presents and Prizes

DOLLAR STORES

Stores like Odd Lot, Family Dollar, Dollar Store, Job Lot, and
Marc's have incredible deals. If you have one of these stores in
your area or something similar, you will definitely want to
make a pit stop for potty party supplies. This is a great place to
find theme underwear or books at very reasonable prices.
Stores like these get new items all the time; keep checking back
to see the new merchandise.

A boot camp mom found some squares of remnant ceramic

tile for next to nothing, and she and her child painted their own trivets and made imprints of their hands. It was their keepsake to remind them of all the fun they had on potty party day.

HOBBY AND CRAFT STORES

Stores like A. C. Moore, Hobby Lobby, Michael's, or the Rag Shop are bursting with all kinds of possibilities. You'll find lots of the items on your shopping list at hobby and craft stores.

One boot camp mom made her own soap from supplies at Michael's and inserted duck erasers inside the transparent glycerin soap bars. This matched her "Bathroom of Wonder" zoo theme, with washcloths and a shower curtain with animal prints and squirting rubber duckies from Wal-Mart.

ORIENTAL TRADING COMPANY

This catalogue is stuffed with hundreds of everyday and theme items you can use as random prizes or items you can make with your child during activities: beach stuff, sports and animal novelties, crafts, and party supplies. If you want it, they have it. This might be one of the kitschiest catalogues you'll ever receive, but it's brimming with some of the best prices on prizes and party decor out there. Call 800-228-2269 or visit www.orientaltrading.com.

TOILET TRAINING TARGETS

Have a little fun while encouraging your child on the potty with flushable potty targets.

Piddlers Toilet Targets: "Foam" fish made from cornstarch and dyed with food coloring.

Toilet-Time Targets: Animal shapes of layered color tissue paper.

Sinkems: Dissolving fun-shaped toilet training targets for boys and girls.

Cheerios Cereal: Moms have been using Cheerios for years with great success.

You can also type "toilet targets" in a search engine and find lots of other brands online.

bibliography

Books

Azrin, Nathan H., Ph.D., and Richard M. Foxx, Ph.D. *Toilet Training in Less Than a Day.* New York: Pocket Books, 1974.

Brazelton, T. Berry, Ann C. Stadtler, and Peter A. Gorski. "Toilet Training Methods, Clinical Interventions, and Recommendations." *Pediatrics* 103:6 (1359). June 1999: 144–145.

Ellison, Sarah. "Un-Pampered: Tots Face Strict Deadline On Toilet-Training." *The Wall Street Journal Online.* August 27, 2004.

Hogg, Tracy, with Melinda Blau. *Secrets of the Baby Whisperer for Toddlers.* New York: Ballantine Books, 2001.

Kagan, Jerome, and Susan B. Gall, editors. *The Gale Encyclopedia of Childhood and Adolescence.* Detroit, Mich.: Gale Research, 1998.

Krueger, Anne, with the editors of *Parenting* magazine. *PARENTING Guide to Toilet Training.* New York: Ballantine Books, 2001.

Lansky, Vicki. *Toilet Training: A Practical Guide to Daytime and Nighttime Training.* Minnetonka, Minn.: Book Peddlers, 1984, 1993, 2002.

Leach, Penelope, Ph.D. "Development and Discipline." *Child,* December 2003–January 2004.

Schaeffer, Charles E., Ph.D., and Theresa Foy DiGeronimo. *Toilet Training Without Tears.* New York: Signet Books, 1989, 1997.

Shelov, Steven, M.D., and Robert E. Hannemann, M.D., editors. *Caring for Your Baby and Young Child,* rev. ed. New York: Bantam, 1998.

Stafford, Diane, and Jennifer Shoquist, M.D. *Potty Training for Dummies.* New York: Wiley Publishing Inc., 2002.

Sonna, Linda, Ph.D. *The Everything Potty Training Book.* Avon, Mass.: Adams Media Corporation, 2003.

Tilton, Sarah. "Testing Diaper-Disposal Devices." *The Wall Street Journal Online.* September 28, 2004.

Wolraich, Mark L., M.D., F.A.A.P., editor in chief with Sherill Tippins. *The American Academy of Pediatrics Guide to Toilet Training.* New York: Bantam Dell, 2003.

acknowledgments

I've been blessed to have a family of cheerleaders behind me, which started with my immediate family and has gained momentum and friends as the years passed. Thanks to each and every one of you for your thoughts, prayers, and support during this entire process.

I want to express my sincerest appreciation to my coauthor, Toni Robino, for bringing her writing expertise to this wonderful project. You are truly one of the most creatively brilliant people I have ever known. Thank you for going above and beyond.

I am infinitely grateful to the people who have helped me negotiate the new terrain of the publishing world: my editor, Nancy Hancock, and Sarah Peach, Marcia Burch, Kelly Bowen, Nancy Inglis, and Debra Model; my agents, Michael Broussard and Jennifer Holder, from Dupree/Miller and Associates.

To Alan Kaufman, Esq., my publishing attorney, and Dale Caldwell, my photographer, I am forever grateful for your generosity.

To those who made contributions to the book, thank you for your expertise: Alan Brightman, Ph.D., Cinda Chima, R.D., Howard Bennett, M.D., Timothy Culbert, M.D., and most important, Philip Caravella, M.D. (you truly are a shining star).

A very big thank-you to Matt and Shari of HGTV's *Room by Room* for their fun, festive, and creative decorating ideas for the potty parties!

Extra-big thanks go to John Ettorre and Mary Pat Sullivan, my proposal doctors. I am eternally grateful for the time you both spent helping me fine-tune and edit my thoughts. John, you are a true gentleman; Mary Pat, you're my angel.

Heidi Dolan and Terri Banks from BABIES R US, thank you for all the opportunities you both have afforded me: hosting my Potty-Training Boot Camps, introducing me to the world of toddler toilet-training products, and allowing me to use your toilet-training paraphernalia. Heidi, your knowledge of toddler products is amazing.

To the Lungo family: Michele for your creativity and contribution to the potty parties, Michael for helping me maintain the website, and Natalie for being my muse.

I appreciate beyond words all the families who over the years have given me the opportunity to be part of their children's toilet-training experience and for allowing me to share their stories.

Thanks to the good folks at the Avon Lake Public Library, especially Nadge Herceg, Sally Klepper, and Paula Shandler, for all their research and recommendations.

And last, but definitely not least, to the best, funniest, and most loving and understanding man in the world, my husband, Kyle: Thanks for letting me renegotiate our parenting agreement. And to my son Spencer, what can I say? I'm crazy about you!

index

about the author

Teri currently lives in Avon Lake, Ohio, with her husband, Kyle, and their son, Spencer. To arrange for speaking engagements or share your success stories, please visit Teri at www.teri crane.com.